D0712748

MEMOIRS OF A MUHINDI

Memoirs of a Muhindi

Fleeing East Africa for the West

MANSOOR LADHA

© 2017 Mansoor Ladha

All rights reserved. No part of this work covered by the copyrights hereon may be reproduced or used in any form or by any means—graphic, electronic, or mechanical—without the prior written permission of the publisher. Any request for photocopying, recording, taping or placement in information storage and retrieval systems of any sort shall be directed in writing to Access Copyright.

Printed and bound in Canada at Marquis. The text of this book is printed on 100% post-consumer recycled paper with earth-friendly vegetable-based inks.

Cover and text design: Duncan Campbell, University of Regina Press
Copy editor: Alison Jacques
Proofreader: Kristine Douaud
Cover photo: David Hurn "Ugandan Asians arrive from Uganda. 1972 G.B. England. London. Heathrow Airport."

Library and Archives Canada Cataloguing in Publication
Ladha, Mansoor, author
Memoirs of a muhindi : fleeing East Africa for the West / Mansoor Ladha.

Issued in print and electronic formats.
ISBN 978-0-88977-474-2 (hardcover).—ISBN 978-0-88977-475-9 (PDF).
—ISBN 978-0-88977-476-6 (HTML)

1. Ladha, Mansoor. 2. Journalists—Canada—Biography.
3. Muslims—Canada—Biography. 4. Immigrants—Canada—Biography.
5. Persecution—Africa, East. 6. Africa, East—Politics and government.
7. Africa, East—Social conditions. I. Title.

PN4913.L33A3 2017 070.92 C2017-900245-7 C2017-900246-5

University of Regina Press
Saskatchewan, Canada, S4S 0A2
TEL: (306) 585-4758 FAX: (306) 585-4699
web: www.uofrpress.ca

10 9 8 7 6 5 4 3 2 1

We acknowledge the support of the Canada Council for the Arts for our publishing program. We acknowledge the financial support of the Government of Canada. / Nous reconnaissons l'appui financier du gouvernement du Canada. This publication was made possible through Creative Saskatchewan's Creative Industries Production Grant Program.

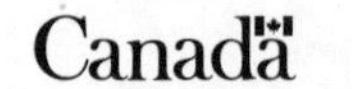

This book is dedicated to the people
of Tanzania for their support
and friendship during my early years
and
to the people of Canada for accepting
immigrants, minorities, and refugees
and allowing them to make their
new homes in Canada.

Diaspora

IF YOU CALL YOURSELF A FRENCH-CANADIAN, INDO-Canadian, Irish-Canadian, German-Canadian, Chinese-Canadian, African-Canadian, or any other hyphenated-Canadian, then you are part of the worldwide diaspora.

In Greek, the word diaspora means "to scatter," but today we use the term to describe a community of people who live outside their shared country of origin or ancestry but maintain active connections with it. A diaspora includes both emigrants and their descendants. While some people lose their attachment to their ancestral homeland, others maintain a strong connection to a place their ancestors may have left generations ago.

Over the last forty-five years, the number of people living outside their country of origin has almost tripled—from 76 million to more than 232 million. More than 3 percent of the world's population now lives outside of the country where they were born. If migrants made up a single nation, it would be the fifth largest in the world.

—*International Diaspora Engagement Alliance (adapted)*

CONTENTS

Preface

DURING MY LAST YEARS IN AFRICA, ASIANS WERE INCREASingly scared to put their thoughts on paper for fear of reprisal. "Tomorrow they will come and put us in jail" was a commonly stated fear. The British colonial authorities didn't encourage freedom of speech, but following independence the situation became worse. When African governments took over, they established one-party systems, banning other political parties—a clear indication they didn't want any alternative views.

Today, most of these African-born Asians reside in Western countries, where they enjoy freedom of speech under charters of rights. Their contribution to our democratic discourse, however, is slowly and gradually disappearing. The Asians who were forced to flee colonial Africa are dying with each passing year. The stories of what they lived through, what they had to give up for freedom, are being lost. Therefore, those of us who are left, we old-timers, need to share our experiences, our persecution, our knowledge—it is our history.

As a group, Asians in East Africa kept to themselves and were a close-knit community. The three-tiered British colonial order kept the races segregated in schools and in residential areas: the British on top, the Asians in the middle, and the black Africans at the bottom; socially, the three peoples hardly interacted before independence.

Many Asians also do not drink alcohol—often a prerequisite to social intermingling in a modern society. In East Africa, cocktail parties at sunset, or sundowners, were common among government departments, diplomatic embassies, and private companies. Hence, Asians were left out of the inner circle of the decision-making echelons of society. Also, among the Asians, Muslims are forbidden to eat pork, while Hindus do not eat beef—additional social barriers.

But despite these handicaps, the sons and daughters of the coolies who built the railways in Africa, the Asian entrepreneurs who opened up the interior, and the traders whose spirit of free enterprise brought them to the shores of Zanzibar made an immense contribution as a whole. The result—a thriving and prosperous

Asian community in East Africa—was the envy of the African majority.

Despite their contribution, economically and commercially, it is unfortunate that no matter how hard they tried, no matter how strong their urge to belong, that desire remained unfulfilled and the Asians had to leave the countries where many of them had been born. No matter how hard they tried to identify themselves with the countries of their birth, to build bridges and seek oneness with the Africans, their brown skin—and perhaps their success—got in the way. The Africans rejected the Asians, viewing them with suspicion and prejudice. Despite perhaps having lived in East Africa for generations, they were seen as people without a country, without a home.

Not much is written about East Africa's Asians by East African–born Asian writers. As such, there is a need for us to write about our experiences in Africa, our accounts of our childhood, our community, and the hardships our ancestors and our families had to undergo.

Thus, as an East African Asian, and especially as a journalist, I felt compelled to write my memoirs, to tell the story of a descendant of immigrants, brown in colour, living in a black society (Tanzania), who later became a brown immigrant living in a white society (Canada). I hope to shed light on the experiences felt by immigrants, the challenges of cross-cultural differences, the hurt of discrimination, and other hardships of displacement.

Most books on Africa inevitably have a political theme, and usually they are written against a backdrop of upheaval, poverty, and violence. As someone born in Africa, I'll never forget my childhood, my neighbourhoods, my school, my classmates, my friends, and my teachers. I loved Tanzania and was willing to die for it, but the circumstances to stay were not in my favour and, regrettably, I had to leave the country of my birth. However, the love for my motherland will live with me forever. As they say, despite everything, a man never forgets where he was born.

As a friend graciously offered, my personal story "illuminates the larger political and cultural backdrop of the so-called post-colonial period in Africa." Yes, what follows is a memoir, but the best memoir brings not merely a life to the page but also the surrounding historical and cultural forces that moved that life. A memoir is at its best when that personal-within-the-historical balance is kept in ways that make it both compelling (because we empathize with the storyteller) and informative (because the personal story is also the story of nations and people in a particular time and place). I hope I have succeeded in discharging that duty.

Acknowledgements

I AM INDEBTED TO VARIOUS PEOPLE WHO CONTRIBUTED directly or indirectly to the making of this book. To my late uncle, Kassamali Ladha, my sisters, Anar and Nasim, and my brothers, Shiraz and Mehboob (Meb), I say thank you. I appreciate your contribution. Thanks also to my son, Hanif, who acted as my first editor and with whom I was able to bounce ideas back and forth. I am also grateful to my wife, Anaar, for allowing me to write and conduct research while I locked myself in the study for hours on end or went to the library.

I am indebted as well to my former classmate and friend Ashok Patel, who studied with me at the Lindi Indian Public School in Tanzania, for providing material for the chapter on Lindi. I also must acknowledge that earlier versions of some chapters and various excerpts have been previously published in my regular columns in the *Calgary Herald* and *Vancouver Sun* newspapers.

My sincere thanks also go to editor David McLennan, managing editor Donna Grant, and copy editor Alison Jacques for their insightful comments and sharp editing. *Asante sana*, David, Donna, and Alison. (Thanks very much.)

Lastly, some of the names in this book have been deliberately changed to safeguard those individuals' privacy, and it is my hope I have not embarrassed anyone.

Colonial Africa

THE PHONE RANG IN THE MIDDLE OF THE NIGHT, DISturbing the silence in the three-storey building in the Malindi area of Zanzibar. Who could it be at this time of the night? It could be bad news.

Nervously, he picked up the receiver from his bedside table: "Hello."

"Count Sahib, *mubaraki* [Count Sir, congratulations]. You have a grandson," the matron of Jessa Bhaloo Maternity Home in Zanzibar said, congratulating my grandfather, Count Ebrahim Ladha. My grandfather was extremely pleased at the news. He had waited for this moment for a very long time. Any hopes and dreams he'd had of an heir for his little kingdom had been unfulfilled due to the lack of a male offspring. Several years after my parents' marriage, I was later told, the matter was so crucial that my grandmother had even suggested that Dad divorce my mom and remarry in order to produce an heir.

However, as it turned out, a grandson was born—six years after the marriage of Hassanali, his oldest son and my father, to beautiful Zera, my mother. And that grandson, born on March 3, 1943, was me. Grandfather was so pleased that, in his excitement, he woke up everyone in the household to give them the news.

"Sorry to wake you up, but I couldn't wait till morning," he announced as he went from room to room, floor to floor, to give the good tidings to each member of the family personally. There was music and jubilation in the Ladha household.

Grandfather was a remarkable man. Born in 1884 in Kutch, India, he decided at the age of twenty to escape the poverty of the Indian village where he grew up—Bhadreshwar, in Gujarat—and immigrated to Zanzibar, East Africa, to seek his fortune. The voyage in those days was not easy. Travellers had to sail in Arab dhows for almost a month before they reached the shores of Africa from India. Some died en route, but most made it and persevered in their quest for a better life. Grandpa started out working for someone else, but eventually he set up his own business, exporting cloves overseas.

My dad ended up working in the thriving and successful family business, while my mom was a housewife, bringing up the kids. It appeared as if I broke the spell on Mom and Dad because there were four more additions to the family after me: two sisters and two brothers.

Grandfather held a *shambo* (communal feast) to celebrate my birth, inviting the Ismaili community for a free lunch. Ismailis—for those who do not know—are a branch of Shia Muslims and followers of the Aga Khan. Today, they number approximately fifteen million and reside primarily in India, Pakistan, Afghanistan, Tajikistan, Europe, North America, and Africa.

My grandfather was a leading and highly regarded member of our community. Many people came to him for advice and guidance on personal and business matters. The whole community attended the *shambo* and were fed *biryani* (rice with spicy meat) and Indian sweets such as *ladoos*, *jalabi*, and *khathyas*. After the meal, everyone enjoyed performing *dandiya raas* and *garba* (traditional Indian dances originating in Gujarat), and the evening ended with a concert by local singers. Everyone had so much fun that they left hoping the count's daughter-in-law would have a second child soon so that he would host another feast!

There was discussion among family members about the name of the new baby, but no agreement was reached. When grandfather heard about it, he called a family meeting. "You people have been wasting time searching for the baby's name. I have a good solution that, I hope, will be acceptable to everyone," he said, amid complete silence in the room. "Prince Aly Khan will be visiting Zanzibar soon. Why don't we ask him to name the baby?"

Everyone looked at him in utter amazement. "What a splendid idea," someone said. "Why didn't we think of that?" Everyone was relieved, as if a huge burden was off their shoulders, and they agreed that they should ask the prince, the father of the present Aga Khan, to name the baby—me—during his forthcoming visit.

Ours was a happy household with a lot of joy, but as the family grew, Dad was forced to seek bigger quarters. We moved four houses down the road from my grandfather's house. Being the oldest child in the family, I remember when my younger siblings cried in the middle of the night. At times it was a chaotic household for my poor mother, who, despite having a helper, had to cope with rearing four children. She was worn out from nursing, feeding, and changing, but somehow she managed without any complaint. Our house was a three-storey building that contained several rooms and dark, long stairs leading to each floor. As children we were often scared that ghosts might be lurking under those dark stairs—the belief in ghosts was prevalent in Zanzibar—however, it was a perfect location for hide and seek.

Zanzibar, an exotic island in the Indian Ocean, became the hub of the first Nizari Ismaili immigrants, who had come mainly from the Bhadreshwar, Kutch, Kathiawar, Surat, and Mumbai areas of India beginning in the 1880s. It became a favourite place for Indian settlers because Zanzibar's Sultan Said, realizing the great potential of Indian immigrants, had adopted a favourable immigration policy.

The majority of the Asian settlers came to East Africa on their own, motivated primarily by their ambitions of seeking better lives for themselves and driven by the spirit of free enterprise. Their main purpose was to trade, and from Zanzibar they moved into the most remote areas of central East Africa, opening up small general stores known as *duka*s—a term derived from the Indian word *dukan*, meaning "a shop." This army of Asian merchants, who came to be known as *dukawalla*s, was largely responsible for the opening of the eastern interior of the continent and for creating a demand for imported goods and helping to spread the use of money. As soon as a lone Asian shopkeeper arrived in the middle of nowhere and opened his store, more families arrived, goods were demanded, and business activity flourished.

Life in colonial Africa was comfortable and peaceful. However, the education system, social clubs, and recreational areas all functioned along racial lines—with the best going to the whites. There was little intermingling of the three races except at the employer-employee level. No one questioned the system, as it was the accepted way of life. Every Asian growing up in colonial Africa went about his or her business, reasonably satisfied with the arrangement.

In Tanganyika, where my family eventually settled, the whites had their exclusive, upscale residential areas. In Dar es Salaam, the capital, this area was called Oyster Bay. Each house there was a mansion overlooking the Indian Ocean. The whites enjoyed the sea breeze while sitting in their beautiful gardens, or beside their swimming pools, while at the iron gates at the entrances to their homes there was an *askari*—a watchman—to prevent prowlers from entering. They created a virtual tropical paradise for themselves, and almost all had several servants. The whites and the upper-class Asians never made their own beds, washed dishes, or weeded gardens. Some butchers even carried "boy's meat"—bones and gristle, meant for the servants—while the masters bought sirloins for themselves.

The racial hierarchy also prevailed in workplaces. In a bank, for example, the boss was usually a white man, while his subordinates—clerks, tellers, and accountants—were Asians, and the cleaners and messengers were Africans. While the Asians could play tennis in European clubs, they were not allowed to enter the club premises for a drink after their games.

In Dar es Salaam, many Asians lived in downtown apartments, close to their businesses, while others lived in suburban areas such as Upanga or Changombe. Asians preferred to live in apartments—or "flats," as we called them. This was especially the case with the Ismailis, who built communal cooperative housing. Ismailis were completely self-sufficient: they were born in an Ismaili maternity home or hospital, were educated in the Aga Khan Ismaili schools, spent their evenings playing sports in Aga Khan clubs, and were buried in their own Ismaili communal cemetery. The Ismailis were a nation in themselves. From the time they were born until they died, they were well served by their communal institutions.

The Africans, or the blacks, lived in Third World conditions in mud or thatched houses with poor sanitation and hardly any plumbing. The area behind Kariakoo, the city's central market district, was allocated for African settlement during colonial times. The Africans stayed in their shantytowns, drinking *pombe*—cheap African liquor—and would often gather around a fire in the centre of the compound in the evenings while someone played drums for entertainment. There was no official colour bar as such, but throughout East Africa areas were zoned by race. It was an accepted way of life. In Nairobi, Kenya, to give one example, Africans lived in Pumwani, Asians in Parkland and Nairobi West, and whites in the suburbs of Muthaiga, Lavington, Karen, and Kitisuru. In pre-independence time, there were even signs on public toilets stating explicitly that certain facilities were reserved for "Europeans Only," "Asians Only," and "Africans Only." Needless to say, the Africans had the worst type.

In Dar es Salaam, the whites enjoyed their evenings at the Gymkhana Club, playing golf, drinking gin and tonic, smoking cigars, reading British newspapers flown in especially for them, discussing British politics or sports, oblivious of—or at least turning a blind eye towards—the realities of Tanganyika's downtrodden masses.

The Asians also had their own communal clubs, such as the Patel Brotherhood, Lohana, and Aga Khan clubs, where they would pass their time playing volleyball or cricket or would enjoy drinking a beer or two, also ignoring African sensitivities. Asian families patronized the Naaz or Purnima restaurants in downtown Dar es

Salaam most evenings, usually concluding with a visit to the Indian paan house.

The paan shop, which often doubled as a tobacconist and place to exchange gossip, was one of the most distinctive features of Dar es Salaam's Asian area. Paan is essentially a dessert consisting of chopped nuts, syrup, and white lime, which are then wrapped in *mtambuu*, or betel leaf. Paan is chewed and sucked but not swallowed. One would pop the triangular parcel into the mouth, munch it, and then spit out the pith when finished.

Every Sunday, carloads of Asian families would head out on picnics, attend drive-in cinemas, or simply go for a drive in Dar es Salaam for pleasure. During such outings with my family in the early 1960s, I would take the wheel. Dad would sit beside me in front, and Mom and my two sisters would sit in the back seat listening to Bollywood songs. We would cruise the seashore, pass through affluent Oyster Bay, and then head back into town for kabobs and tea at the Naaz, where we didn't even have to get out of the car as service was provided on a tray hung from the vehicle's window. These outings were a part of most Asian families' weekly rituals.

Asians were generally considered bad employers in East Africa, said to overwork their employees, underpay them, and give them no overtime wages. There were no strict labour standards, and servants—who were often fed a family's leftover food—washed clothes, did the dishes and the beds, cleaned toilets, polished shoes, dusted, and vacuumed, along with anything else that needed to be done. Some of these domestic workers started early in the morning and worked till six or seven o'clock in the evening; they sometimes had to work weekends and holidays. This system continued for years, and it was practised especially among the older generation of Asian employers. It was a colonial system, functioning with neither labour laws nor a minimum-wage structure.

The life of an African domestic servant was terrible. Most of them would come from rural areas, travelling into the city by bus or on foot to work. The *ayahs* (nannies) were hired to look after babies, while male servants were hired to do household chores. In some households, loyal servants would work their whole life for a particular family, looking after the same master, his children, and his grandchildren. When a servant got old, he would recommend his son or a close relative as his replacement.

As I've said, the three races—Africans, Asians, and Europeans—lived in separate worlds, though things were not as bad in East Africa as in apartheid South Africa. We had separate schools, hospitals, and residential areas, and this was accepted. We were born with it. This institutionalized prejudice was the law under the colonial system, and we Asians never felt anything was wrong with the arrangement. Until after independence. It was only when the tables were turned, and we were discriminated against by the black population, that we Asians began to realize that we hadn't treated the Africans fairly or as equals. This awakening came especially among the younger, progressive, and educated Asians, who tried to improve the situation in their own little ways.

* * *

Tanganyika, colonized by Germans in the mid-1880s, and a part of German East Africa after 1891, became a British territory after the First World War. It attained independence from British rule in 1961 and merged with the island of Zanzibar in 1964 to become Tanzania.

When *uhuru* (independence) was on the horizon, it meant different things to different people. *Uhuru* to the white and brown citizens meant an end to their racial superiority. It meant a threat to their property, to their privileged way of life, and an end to their concept of themselves as masters of the oppressed black race. To the Africans, it meant power—power to manage, or mismanage, the way they wanted to rule their country and to make decisions affecting their fate and their future. African animosity towards Asians brewed as independence drew nearer, and the Asians became increasingly wary of the repercussions.

"We are going to be in charge," the Africans would say, and servants were openly defiant to their employers. "We are going to be *bwana kubas* (big bosses) whether you like it or not. Wait till we take control. Now you guys will be our servants. We will take over your homes, businesses, motor cars, and even your beautiful daughters."

As the oldest child in our family, I was frightened to hear this kind of talk. I had two younger sisters who would need to be protected, so, unknown to the rest of the family, I kept my brother's hockey stick close to my bed. I vowed to protect the family's honour if need be. In those days, Asians were not allowed to keep guns; that was a privilege accorded to Europeans only. But I was too young to own a gun anyway.

Rashida and Rukhsana, two pretty Asian girls in our neighbourhood, even received marriage proposals from African suitors who openly told them that they would marry them after independence, whether the girls liked it or not. The men started bidding on them as if they were some kind of chattel.

Juma, our faithful servant, reported people in the market saying that all the goods from the Asians' *duka*s would be divided and distributed among the Africans and, likewise, the white farmers' sheep and cattle would also be taken and distributed. "Those Asians and white people who did not want to stay under black rule will either be killed or driven into the sea," Juma reported dutifully—adding, "and there will be plenty of *pombe* (alcohol) for everybody to enjoy."

Whenever Juma was in a good mood, he would tell me that he fantasized about a vivacious and pretty Goan girl, Mary, who lived next door. Mary was in the habit of sunbathing on the deck in her bikini and occasionally would take off her top. Whenever Juma got an erection while seeing her topless, he would find a convenient and quiet corner to masturbate. He declared that he desired to have Mary as his proud possession come Independence Day.

There were some hard-core Asians who just couldn't accept the country's impending independence. Habib Gangji, a prominent Asian merchant and owner of several properties, was sitting in his air-conditioned building in Dar es Salaam's Mnazi Mmoja area when he heard the news on the radio. He couldn't digest the fact that these "primitive" Africans—whom he had been calling "boy" and *gollas* or *karias* (derogatory terms Asians used to call Africans) all his life—would be rulers and masters.

"My ancestors have moulded and nurtured the commerce of this country," he explained. "Am I going to give the keys of my thriving business and properties to an African who until yesterday was climbing trees picking coconuts? Is my granddaughter Shamim going to marry one of these African boys because they have had British education? No way. *Gollas* will be *gollas!*"

Gangji continued, "I blame all this entirely on the British. The *mzungu* [white man] never did his homework. I mean, look at Ghana, the first country to become independent in Africa under Nkrumah. The country is in a mess. The British are too quick to grant *uhuru* to their African colonies. These Africans don't know how to govern. They will not be able to drive us out of the country because they won't be able to do without us. We, the Asians, have opened up the interior of Africa. Our *duka*s made them use oil, kerosene, soap, and clothing; otherwise, they would be roaming around naked. We are the pioneers who have contributed immensely to the development of the country.

"Look at the Belgian Congo. What a mess Patrice Lumumba, the Russian lackey, and Kasavubu made there! Those shameless Africans even raped the nuns," he pointed out. "No, this will not happen here in Tanganyika. Not in my lifetime. *Uhuru* to the Africans would mean a license to rob and steal, to kill without punishment, and I am convinced the British will not allow it."

Independence Day finally arrived on December 9, 1961, and human nature being what it is, blacks in Tanganyika sought vengeance against their white and brown "oppressors." In upcountry stations, lootings of Asian shops and break-ins were reported. Some Africans expected independence to bring instant prosperity, believing that the breaking of colonial bonds would bring a wave of expected benefits—high wages, good homes, vehicles.

When independence did finally come, everything changed at once. The pyramid structure we were so used to changed abruptly: the Africans were now on top, the Europeans were in the middle, and the Asians were suddenly at the bottom. A revolution had taken place. Friends became enemies, people looked over their shoulders wondering if they would be attacked, and employers wondered whether or not to trust their employees.

The racial animosity brewing during the late colonial period continued during and after independence. It was at this time that writer Paul Theroux made the blunt observation that "everyone in East Africa hates Asians."[1] Often called the "Jews of East Africa" for their dominance of trade and commerce, the Asians were a favourite target of verbal attacks. At political rallies and in Parliament, African politicians saw the Asians as an easy punching bag, and the masses clapped along to their jabs with enthusiasm.

Theroux identified the British colonialists as those responsible for spreading this hatred. "The British have hated the Asians the longest," he said. "This legacy they passed on to the Africans who, now in Kenya for example, hold the banner of bigotry high. Political scientists, anthropologists and sociologists in Africa largely ignore the Asian community. That students in East African universities hate Asians is a demonstrable fact. . . . Racial insult against Asians now approaches the proportion of a fashion," he added.

Describing the Asians as the "most lied about race in Africa," Theroux further claimed Africans saw the *muhindi* (a Swahili word to describe people of Asian descent) as being responsible for "flagrant racism, the failure of African socialism and progress, all the bad driving and motor accidents, sins of pride, envy, scandal, gluttony and lust, monopoly business, African neurosis, subversion of ruling parties, the success of such dissident parties as the Kenya People's Union, the bloodshed of such terrorist groups as the shifta, a high birth rate and bad food."[2]

Not only did everyone hate the Asians, according to Theroux, but even Asians themselves hated other Asians.

Now, why would Asians hate their own race, their own people? The only explanation I can put forward is that East Africa's Asians were under British colonial authority for such a long time that they formed an inferiority complex about themselves. But while we Asians always felt inferior to the white ruling class, we must remember that we weren't on the lowest rung of the colonial social ladder.

The full realization that we were not wanted in Africa came to us—the whole Asian community—in 1972 when Ugandan dictator Idi Amin expelled the country's eighty thousand Indians, Pakistanis, and Ugandan Asians, apparently after receiving a message from God in his dreams. It was a bombshell. This dream of Amin's became a nightmare for Uganda's Asians—the majority of whom had been in the country for three generations. They were given ninety days to leave the country. This ethnic cleansing soon spread to neighbouring Kenya and Tanzania, where discrimination and property grabs went largely unnoticed by the international media, and many families lost everything.

Asian households began holding family meetings to evaluate their future in Africa. My family also held a meeting, and although we considered Tanzania our homeland, the time had come to make serious decisions in light of the changing political landscape. Amin had provided a wake-up call, and day by day the socialist-leaning Tanzanian president Julius Nyerere was making it difficult for Asians to make a living as a business community.

And things weren't looking better next door. Immigration laws in neighbouring Kenya were becoming increasingly draconian. Foreigners were permitted to hold a job only until a Kenyan national could be found to replace them. There were also more and more demands urging the government to ban non-Kenyans from owning a shop or trading in municipal markets. Asians were having difficulty surviving due to the government's Africanization policies, which guaranteed jobs for Africans.

Dad was furious when a property he owned was nationalized without any compensation because he was classified as a *mirija* (exploiter/bloodsucker) in accordance with the prevalent socialist jargon. And he was frustrated with not being able to get any supplies for his business while, at the same time, our philosopher president was busy translating Shakespeare's *Julius Caesar* into Swahili. As such, our family assembled in our lavish living room after dinner one day to discuss our future. After looking at various options, it was decided my younger brother and his wife, both medical doctors, and myself, a senior journalist, should consider leaving for England, Canada, or the United States. Fortunately, one of my two sisters was already in the United States, and the other had settled in London, England, so we didn't have to worry about them. The fifth sibling, my youngest brother, was still in high school.

Canada was at the top of our list due to the personal friendship between then Canadian prime minister Pierre Trudeau and the Aga Khan—a friendship that greatly facilitated the easy entry of Ismailis and other Asians into the country. England, with whom Ismailis and other Asians had close ties because of its colonial legacy, was considered less desirable because of its already-large existing immigrant population from other former colonies and the mounting racial animosity towards non-white immigrants. This was also the time when Conservative MP Enoch Powell made his infamous "Rivers of Blood" speech, bringing the issue of non-white immigration to the forefront.

I decided to leave Tanzania soon after 1970 when Nyerere nationalized the *Standard*, the country's leading English newspaper, where I then worked. I had a falling-out with the newly appointed editor, Fred Ngunga, who bypassed my promotion, as I'll discuss later, in favour of a black person. This hurt me tremendously. I had stood for fairness with an unblemished record of selflessness while at university, and I had also been a *mwanainchi* (compatriot)—a very nationalistic person in my young adult life.

My inner voice began to question my allegiance to my country; it told me that I had been a fool for being loyal to Tanzania. I knew other Asians, too, felt they were being victimized and abandoned. It became apparent that whatever we did, however faithful and loyal we tried to be to what we felt was our homeland, Asians were not accepted in Africa.

The straw that broke the camel's back for me was the establishment of a rule that all staff at the paper had to become members of the ruling party, the Tanzania African National Union, if they wanted to keep their jobs. The new regulation didn't make much sense; after all, Tanzania was a one-party state, where opposition parties were banned. Only two daily English newspapers were published in the country: the *Standard* (later renamed the *Daily News*), which was now owned by the government, and the *Nationalist*, owned by the country's only political party. To work as a journalist in English print media, one had to work with one of these two newspapers, both of which were closely tied by ownership to the government.

The majority of the local staff had little choice but to take out party membership, but I couldn't convince myself to do this; I firmly believed that my employment at the paper existed because I was a good journalist and not because I was holding the party's membership card. I also believed that a journalist should be independent and non-partisan, affiliated with no political party. It was time to leave my beloved country.

This was a period of complete upheaval in the lives of most Asians. We felt unwanted and abandoned; our desire to live in harmony with the Africans was rejected. We felt alienated, our citizenship was downgraded, our possessions were taken over, and our sense of our right to belong was very much questioned.

Who in their right mind would stay under these harsh conditions? The only option was to leave the country we had cherished so much. This marked the beginning of the Asian diaspora from Africa, our flight to the West.

Under precarious circumstances, we had to make some tough choices about our future. Would our decision to leave be the right one? We would ask ourselves this question often.

As in the movies, I could see my happy childhood in Africa flashing in front of me. I could then see turbulent events unfolding, the racial tensions, the sowing of the seeds of revolution that would force us to flee.

Lindi

DAD WORKED FOR SMITH MACKENZIE & COMPANY, WHICH was both a clearing and forwarding company and a shipping agency. Mom ran a clothing store in the front of the house. Dad was a good provider. After a falling-out with his wealthy father in Zanzibar, he left the island, practically penniless, to seek a new life in Lindi, a town in the southern part of what was then Tanganyika. Once he established himself, he made sure we had good clothes, imported food, bikes, and vacations in Zanzibar to visit my grandparents almost every year.

Lindi was one of the oldest towns in the country. It was established by the Arabs, whose culture and religion still dominate the place. During our years there, we watched Lindi grow from a small town of five thousand to one with a population of twelve thousand. New construction—post office, prison, school, public and government offices, quarters for government employees, hospital, market, tarmac roads, bridges, and flourishing businesses—started springing up. We also witnessed the establishment of the only cinema in the whole of Tanganyika's southern province.

There was prosperity everywhere as Lindi became not only a medium-sized administrative town, but also an important government centre for the province under the British. It also had a good school system, drawing students from all over the province; private boarding homes were usually patronized by students from different upcountry areas, while other students stayed with families.

Rivalry always existed between Lindi and Mtwara, a town near the Mozambique border. Mtwara started getting recognition after the government constructed a deep-water berth port there to allow large ships to handle exports arising from the groundnut (peanut) scheme. Although the port remained underutilized, in 1952 the province's main harbour and administrative centre was moved to Mtwara. Although Lindi was again made the regional administrative centre in 1971, it never regained its former economic and educational prominence.

My family lived on the King's African Rifles Street (called KAR Street for short), a middle-class area with bungalows, some with shops in front and living quarters at the back. Our house had three bedrooms, with kitchen and dining facilities and a huge fenced backyard with trees.

The house we lived in had electricity, but the bathroom and toilet were outside, so one had to take a kerosene lamp with them if a trip was necessary during the night. We didn't have running water, but all the houses on the street had wells. Our well was small and not very deep, with a rounded opening at the mouth. As kids, after, say, a football (soccer) game, we would draw its cool and sparkling water up directly and drink it—though Mom always boiled the water for home consumption.

Houses on our street were built of mud plastered on sticks firmly grounded, and were whitewashed inside and outside, finished as elegant bungalows. In addition to residences, KAR Street also had quite a few small shops. Thieves would pour water on a shop's mud walls and then cut through the sticks, making a hole through which to enter the premises, and open the main door, allowing their colleagues to come inside and steal merchandise. They would then load their vehicles, parked outside, while the shopkeeper and his family slept. Many believed that the thieves brought young boys with them so that a smaller hole in the wall was required for entry.

Our shop was broken into twice before we acquired a guard dog, named Tiger, who also became a beloved family pet. Tiger, a German shepherd, did a marvellous job. He would bark at the slightest noise, waking up the whole family; the thieves, realizing there was a ferocious dog not to be messed with, soon crossed our shop off their list of targets.

Tiger was allowed to wander in our enclosed backyard, but when we had company we had to tie him up or he would go berserk seeing so many strange people in the house. Occasions such as birthdays were celebrated with Tiger out of sight, because in his excitement he would jump on guests, placing his front paws on their chests, and children were especially scared of him.

There was much harmony in Lindi between the town's different communities, and we celebrated each other's festivals. One such occasion was Eid Mela, the Muslim festival marking the end of the month of Ramadhan, at which residents of all denominations and races got together for entertainment, games, and food. Everyone in Lindi also participated in Diwali, the Hindu festival of lights, which was celebrated with lots of firecrackers and fireworks displays, and where a Hindu dish called *bhel* was a favourite of most people. During both Eid and Diwali, people dressed in their best clothes. Muslims would dress in Moghul attire, wearing red Egyptian caps and *sarwal khamis*, while young Hindu women looked especially beautiful in their silk saris as they went about distributing sweets to their friends, relatives, and neighbours. On such occasions the town became Little Bombay, with much parading of wealth and religious spectacle.

A weekly ritual that most Asians followed religiously in Lindi was a Sunday outing to the town's only movie theatre, the Novelty Cinema. There were two daily showings of Indian films, one early in the evening and the other at night. Going to the movies is ingrained in the Asian culture and tradition. The fact that Bollywood produces the largest number of films in the world is testimony to that, and going to the movies remains a time when families and friends get together for both entertainment and fellowship.

In those days, when we were kids, all cinema tickets had seat numbers, so many patrons preferred to reserve seats. Patrons fought to get good ones. Season-ticket holders would befriend the ticket clerk, Jayanti, who would hold good seats for these "friends" and for preferred patrons—presumably for a small fee or in return for future favours. Whenever there was a song or a dance sequence in a movie, smokers in the audience, mostly men, would go out for a smoke; this practice was so common that it was not considered unusual at all.

Another Sunday pastime for Lindi residents was to spend evenings walking and sitting on the benches at the seashore, enjoying the breeze off the Indian Ocean. Many Asians, including my parents, enjoyed coming out with the whole family to meet up with their friends to chat, socialize, and drink *madafu* (coconut water). Kids would go for a swim.

As kids, we felt we lived in an invincible age, and we enjoyed a fascinating, innocent, and adventurous childhood. We had no worries, and life was good. We played on the acacia trees on the golf grounds—climbing, swinging, and jumping off—while other times we would go *khungu* picking, using sticks to hit the fruits until they fell off the trees. During the cash crop season, when all crops from the southern province were gathered for export from Lindi, we loved to climb and play on the mountains of piled sacks full of castor oil seeds, groundnuts, dried cassava, maize, beans, and sesame seeds. Sometimes we would pierce a hole or two to get cassava and groundnuts out to eat.

We also played cricket, football, and *gilli-danda* on the streets—*gilli-danda* is an ancient Indian sport, thought to be a forerunner of Western games such as cricket and baseball. But unlike the youths of today, we didn't have the luxury of expensive Nikes, Adidas, or other brand-name shoes to wear when playing sports. Most of the time, we played barefoot.

Nage—a game played with seven stone tablets piled one on another—was also popular. Two teams of seven played, with one player taking a turn as a striker while the others stood behind the pile. The striker would throw a tennis ball with the intention of bringing down the pile of stone tablets, while the opposing team had to regroup the stones and kick the ball off. The fielding team collected the ball and tried to hit the person trying to pile the stones. If they managed to hit the person before the pile was complete, then the team was declared out and the opposing team took its turn.

But by far the favourite sport among most Asians in East Africa was cricket—a legacy of British rule—and today cricket still dominates any other game in India, Bangladesh, Zimbabwe, the Caribbean, and South Africa (all former British colonies). Soccer was preferred by most Africans.

Kids playing cricket usually took every open space in the neighbourhood, and they knew the names of famous cricket players from the West Indies, Britain, and India. Many kids took pride in calling themselves by the name of a favourite team's famous bowler or batsman—some nicknamed themselves after such notables as Garry Sobers, Don Bradman, and Imran Khan.

But while cricket was our passion, all neighbourhood kids would also play soccer, especially on Sunday afternoons. For a skinny guy, I was a good player. I played with my left foot, and my position usually was left centre or centre forward. With my light body, I could run faster than other players and had mastered the art of passing the ball tactfully. The lighter you are, the more agile you become. My skinny body, however, was also a disadvantage: I was often teased and called *gonda* (Swahili for skinny) and was the target of bullies in school. Still, I was always chosen for my school soccer team—that is, until my dad got upset with me because I broke two pairs of glasses, one after the other. Soccer had become an expensive venture.

Whenever our school team played, notices were sent to other classes and players' names were read aloud by the teachers. We were flattered that our names were read in front of girls who were then encouraged to come to watch the games and cheer. I had a crush on a girl who was one class behind me. I made sure she knew when my games were, and she usually attended.

The town's popular soccer stadium, where all cup matches were played, was near our house. Many big political rallies and public functions were also held at this stadium. As Canada thrives on hockey, Tanganyika thrived on soccer. Lindi was a typical soccer town, with teams like the Young Africans (Yanga) or Sunderland (Sanda) among the favourites. Every year, soccer players from different district teams came to the stadium to play matches in the hope of being selected for the Lindi regional team, which would go on to compete against other national teams in Dar es Salaam for the annual Gossage Cup. The Lindi team's centre forward, Akwitende, who was an excellent player, and Tindo, a good defence player, were usually selected to represent the national Tanganyika XI team, which competed against Kenyan and Ugandan teams.

Whenever our teams played, all activities in town would come to a standstill and people would congregate near a radio to listen to commentaries and learn how their favourite teams fared. There was no TV at the time. Everyone in town talked and breathed soccer during the season. Restaurants, bars, and coffee shops did brisk business during every game.

* * *

"*Vande Mataram! Vande Mataram!*" (We bow to you, mother.) At Lindi's primary school, where I began my elementary education, a general assembly was held every morning where all students congregated to sing India's independence song. We sang the song because at the school, named Indian Public School, the majority of students were Hindus. Most of my school friends were Hindu boys, with names like Ashok, Dinesh, Hashwant, and Narendra, and girls with names such as Asha, Indu, and Rohini. Non-Hindu students were expected to attend the morning assemblies and sing the song out of respect, but they also participated in the singing, I like to think, because of its moving and beautiful lyrics.

At Indian Public School we also learned Indian history, about the great Mughal emperors. We learned the romantic story behind the famous Taj Mahal: how the Mughal emperor Shah Jahan built this monument of love in memory of his beloved queen, Mumtaz. These were among my first lessons of the history of the country of my forefathers.

Our coeducational school was the biggest and considered the best school in the whole province. It had started as a two-classroom school, but over time more classrooms were added (with thatched roofs); eventually the school was expanded with more buildings in the rear and a substantial three-storey building to the right. When the school was undergoing construction, students had fun jumping from the top floor of this building to the sand heaps below.

In 1956, a day before our final year-end exams, Lindi was hit by a cyclone. Like most students, I was up early reviewing my lessons when the lights went out. The corrugated sheets on the roof started rattling, and then sheets from all the roofs in our neighbourhood began to fly off and were swept along by the heavy rains and ferocious winds. Rainwater started coming into the house. We had huge tables in the shop, and all of us kids took shelter under the tables to shield ourselves from the downpour. The rains finally subsided after a couple of days.

School officials were forced to postpone the exams for a week. The golf grounds in front of the school were knee-deep in water, and a number of coconut trees had fallen down. We kids took advantage of this, wading in the water to get to the trees, to the coconuts, and finally to our treasure, the *kilele* (the inside of the coconut).

Lindi's Indian Public School had football, table tennis, and field hockey teams. Some of the table tennis players at our school were the best players in the whole province. Our school cricket team was strong as well. We used to play against the whites from Nachingweya—groundnut farmers—and beat them. In those days, beating a white team was considered quite an achievement.

In 1959 the government opened a brand-new secondary school, roughly four miles outside the town. My classmates and I spent our last two years of schooling there before the final exams that marked the end of high school. At this school, we had athletics such as shot-put, javelin, discus, and relay races for the first time. Since the school was some distance from town, most boys bought bicycles to ride back and forth. Boys would often race one another at top speed down a small hill near the school, the result being a number of falls where students hurt themselves, but that was part of life in those days.

In the same year the new school opened, 1959, an exchange visit to Tanga, a coastal city north of Dar es Salaam, was arranged. Our principal, Frank Ranger, had once taught there. Many students, including me, registered to go, but something came up at the last minute and I had to back out. The families of the host students in Tanga had offered to put up each visiting student in their homes, and a whole bus was rented to take the excited Lindi students there. The hosts had arranged a full program of events that included sports activities and athletic events during the daytime, followed by social events and dances in the evenings.

One day during this trip, the students were taken to the famous Pangani waterfalls for a full day of picnicking. Everyone was having a good time near the edge of the falls, and there was a cool breeze. Some of the students seemed to find the setting somewhat romantic, and a few boyfriends and girlfriends vanished into the bushes, away from the teachers' glances. Others simply talked and enjoyed the scenery by the water.

One pretty girl from Lindi asked another Lindi student, Nandu, if he could get her a glass of cold water from the falls. "For sure," said Nandu, who fancied the girl. But instead of just getting water from the nearest point, he went a little distance away—perhaps to obtain the coldest water possible. As he bent over to fill a cup with water, he didn't realize that the stone on which he was standing was very slippery and he slipped right into the surging waterfalls.

Someone shouted that Nandu had fallen into the falls, and all of a sudden there was commotion everywhere. The tranquility of the picnic was shattered, replaced by confusion and anxiety among the students. The principal and other teachers could see Nandu being taken forcefully by the powerful water and, without even thinking, Mr. Ranger threw himself into the falls behind the frightened student. An excellent swimmer, Mr. Ranger soon caught up with Nandu and pushed him towards some bushes, which he was able to hold on to until help arrived and he was taken to safety.

Meanwhile, Mr. Ranger tried frantically to fight the powerful waters of the falls. The students kept looking for his yellow shirt, but he had disappeared into the blue water. A rescue team came and worked as long as the evening light would allow, but Mr. Ranger's body was never recovered. Two days later, the bus returned to Lindi without Mr. Ranger, who had originally planned the trip. Students can be cruel at times, and many expressed their hatred for Nandu quite openly. Some even taunted him to his face, saying it would have been better if he had died instead.

For a few days, there was sadness in the school. A prayer meeting was held for Mr. Ranger's soul, and counselling was provided to students to help them overcome their grief. It was an uneasy time, and Nandu stayed away for several weeks. Despite this tragedy—and the fact that living as colonial subjects was never a good thing, especially since the British colonizers disliked us Asians so much—it must be acknowledged that one of the most cherished fringe benefits of colonialism was a British education. As British subjects we studied in good schools that had qualified teachers, and our papers for the last exam before leaving a secondary school—Standard XII or Senior Cambridge—came all the way from London's Cambridge University. Hence, our qualifications were comparable to those of graduates from an English educational institution. Thanks to that sound colonial British education, many East African Asians were fluent in English, which enabled them to find jobs in Western countries easily, compared with other immigrants. Sound education was the best legacy of colonialism.

As the oldest child in the family, I was well liked by my parents. Mom adored me and sometimes favoured me, to the protestations of my other siblings, but her standard reply was "All of you are equal to me. Both my eyes are the same." Dad used to introduce me to his friends as "my Prince of Wales."

Dad was a simple person who sometimes appeared deep in thought, though he was quite lively when he was with his friends. He was a voracious reader, keeping abreast of international and local news. He enjoyed reading the daily paper. Perhaps it was because of this that I gained my infatuation with newspapers, which led to a career in journalism. Even today, I must read the day's newspaper, even that of whichever country I'm in when on vacation—a habit I have cultivated since childhood, thanks to my dad.

There was no home delivery of the daily paper in Lindi. The paper came by air every day from Dar es Salaam. When it came in the mornings, Dad would pick up a copy from the newsagent on his way to work, while when it came in the evenings I didn't mind going to pick it up on my bike.

Dad always liked walking, so he didn't have a car. He walked to the office and back each day. When I went to university, and was old enough to drive, he bought me a car and I had the distinction of being one of the few students with one. Many of my friends, who were envious of my status as a car owner, borrowed my car for dates with their girlfriends on Saturday evenings. I could have started a small rental business. I am pleased to say that many of those college girls became wives after spending time with their boyfriends in my car—lending my vehicle out was one of my socialist deeds that I am most proud of.

My mother was the timid type, but she was the foundation of the family. All the children would go to her for advice because she was good at counselling. After school, as the oldest, I sometimes had to substitute for her in this capacity while she cooked. Mom was in the habit of singing her favourite song, Lata Mangeshkar's "Mer Man Dole, Mera Tan Dole," while cooking.

Whenever she was sick, we had a potential problem regarding food. In keeping with the prevalent stereotypical tradition in a male-dominated society, Dad didn't know how to cook, nor did he make any attempt to learn. Their roles were straightforward: he was the breadwinner and Mom was the housewife, with a duty to look after the household, which included cooking and rearing the children. But Mom, anticipating being sick at times or being away, would cook enough food for several weeks, marking packages with labels and leaving them in the freezer for us.

The company where my father worked sold imported items, such as canned foods like butter, tinned fruits, and jams, imported from South Africa—the bastion of racism and apartheid at the time. South Africa had enacted apartheid laws institutionalizing racial discrimination in 1948. As an astute and politically conscious high school student, I had a problem consuming these South African products when Dad brought them home, manufactured as they were by a repressive regime. Plucking up courage one day, I told him, "Dad, you know we should not be buying these South African products because by doing so, we are supporting the economy of the apartheid regime, which is so blatantly practising racism and denying human rights to the non-white population.

"By buying their merchandise, we are promoting their regime and encouraging their business," I argued. "South Africa is the enemy of every progressive-minded person. I am going to stop eating these items until you accept my point of view and find an alternative source of goods," I added, hoping to persuade him with my ultimatum.

My father relayed my concerns to his colleagues in the office, and soon it became a big issue. The staff saw the moral of the story and started boycotting South African goods, so much so that the demand for them went down dramatically. The manager was concerned about the drop in business, and he summoned Dad to explain. He accepted Dad's point of view and was forced to seek alternative supplies. I was personally satisfied to have taken this stand against apartheid and for making a small dent in the regime's export market.

* * *

I haven't had an opportunity to visit the town of my upbringing since I left for further education in 1960. In a way it's for the best, because I have good memories of my childhood, the town, and its residents. Those who have been back to Lindi have been saddened by the state in which they have found the place. My former classmate Ashok Patel, now a resident of London, England, has been to Lindi and reported that everything was in ruins.

"The schools are neglected buildings, though still functioning. The Indian Sports Club grounds have been built upon. The stadium lies in ruins with shacks built on it. Roads have been topped up year after year instead of being repaired," he explained. "The government offices (*boma*) have been surrounded by overgrown trees and creepers like the ruins in Far Eastern countries. Businesses are skeletal. A few buildings built by affluent Asians remain.

"The airport is just a strip in a field. The seashores are filling up with sand; the cannons mounted on the sea defence walls have toppled over onto the beach and are buried in sand; and the bridge between the old wharf and the warehouse was washed out in heavy rains. The provincial commissioner and district commissioner quarters are standing in ruins."

Ashok reminisced about Lindi's glorious past. "The heart is heavy now and sad. The mind is full of good memories trying to rebuild the old Lindi! Good to keep in touch with the Lindians of those days. It does give solace to the soul and joy to the heart," he concluded.

Feud and Revolution

DURING SUMMER HOLIDAYS, WE USED TO GO TO ZANZIBAR, via the SS *Mombasa*, which belonged to Smith Mackenzie & Company, where Dad worked. Lindi had no facilities for people to board or disembark, so the ships used to anchor at the far end of the harbour, and passengers were transported back and forth by smaller boats. It was fun to get a first taste of fresh sea breeze as the boat proceeded, filled with more than its passenger carrying capacity and lots of luggage. (As there were no luggage restrictions, passengers could carry as much as they wanted to.) The winds would blow cold, salty sea water from the Indian Ocean onto the faces of passengers sitting on both sides of the boat.

The ship had huge decks below, and it appeared as if the gigantic cranes on the docks were loading goods into the empty stomach of the ship. The cargo was then covered with solid steel beams and tarpaulins. It was very common for many passengers with third-class tickets to spread a blanket or a sleeping bag on the decks, where they would sleep during their two- to three-day journey to Zanzibar. After leaving Lindi, the ship would make a brief stopover at Kilwa, offload passengers and cargo at Dar es Salaam and Zanzibar, and finally end its journey at Mombasa. Then it would start the return trip again from Mombasa to Lindi, which was the last stop. The journey also had a socializing aspect and assumed a festival atmosphere. Groups of four or six passengers would get together and play cards to while away the time. Passengers would make new friends and renew old relationships. Several people would even bring food with them in a *tiffin*—a food container with different compartments—for their journey. During mealtimes the area smelled of food being warmed, making passengers hungry.

We loved to go to Zanzibar, where my grandparents lived. Grandfather had a clove plantation, on which many tropical fruit trees grew. We enjoyed picking fruits, ripe, ready to be eaten, their juices flowing down our chins—fruits like *matufa*, *shoki shoki*, durian, lychee, and others that were grown only in Zanzibar.

My favourite fruit, which is grown in Zanzibar and Southeast Asia, happens to be durian, dubbed the "king of fruits." Durian lovers describe it as a fruit that smells like hell, but tastes like heaven. During a recent visit to Zanzibar, I brought durian to my hotel but had to eat it on a bench outside the premises as its flesh emits a strong and distinctive odour.

Grandpa's plantation also had a fully equipped bungalow, with four bedrooms, a spacious kitchen, a living room, and a huge veranda in front. We usually invited friends to join us for a barbecue and a campfire at night, where we would sit in a circle and sing songs until the wee hours of the morning. When we went to bed, we could hear insects making noise and dogs howling in the distance.

My grandfather was in the habit of drinking strongly brewed *kahawa* (coffee) every morning and afternoon. He was a regular customer of an Arab coffee-seller who kept freshly brewed coffee in a container under a bed of burning charcoal, ensuring that the coffee was always hot and fresh. The coffee-seller serviced our neighbourhood, and everyone who was with my grandfather at the time would get free coffee, courtesy of my grandfather, who paid the guy once a month. It was during those earlier days of my life that I cultivated a taste for strong black coffee, served in tiny cups. People commonly started their day by drinking three or four cups of coffee. Another delicacy of Zanzibar was halva, an Arab sweet wrapped in special basket-like containers and mainly eaten as dessert. To this day, people who visit the island take halva as a present for their friends.

Zanzibar was also our favourite place for another special reason. Our whole family were born in Zanzibar, and my first girlfriend lived in Zanzibar. A fair-skinned blonde with blue eyes, she was many times mistaken for a white girl. Every time I came to Zanzibar, I brought a soccer ball with me. I even became captain of the soccer team there. It certainly was strange that the team's captain came periodically by boat from Lindi for soccer games! My girlfriend was the only girl who also played on our team at the Aga Khan Club—we were perhaps the only soccer team in the world with ten boys and one girl. In Canada, women playing soccer is a recent phenomenon, but we had this girl playing soccer in those days. She definitely drew crowds, and it was such a novelty to see a girl play soccer that they usually cheered for our team.

My grandfather, as one of the most prominent businessmen on the island, had business dealings with the sultan of Zanzibar. During one of my trips to Zanzibar, I indicated a desire to meet the sultan. A few days later, my grandfather phoned the sultan's palace and made an appointment for the following week.

I was excited when the time came. I had seen the sultan and his wife driving by every evening at a set time in a red Rolls Royce and waving to the crowds on the seashore. As a child I had joined with other kids to line the street and wave at the sultan's motorcade; now, to be in his presence, face to face, would be an experience of a lifetime.

On the day of our appointment, I got up early and put on a tie and a blazer. We went to the sultan's palace, which was a huge building on the seashore, close to the famous Baitula Jaib (House of Wonders). My grandfather introduced himself to the *askari* (guard) at the massive iron gate, who was wearing a khaki uniform and holding a rifle. We met the sultan's private secretary in the drawing room. People dressed in dark blue suits were going in and out of adjoining offices, everyone looking smart and very busy. After about ten minutes we were escorted into his presence. There he was sitting on the throne, an Arab gentleman, dressed majestically in a flowing robe, wearing a golden turban, and extending his hand of welcome to my grandfather with a smile.

"Jambo Mzee Ebrahim. Karibu!" he said. (*Mzee* is a salutation used for elderly people.) "Greetings, Mr. Ebrahim. Welcome."

"Thank you, Your Highness," my grandfather replied. "I would like to introduce my grandson, Hassanali's son Mansoor, who has been very anxious to meet you."

I moved forward and extended my hand. The sultan gripped my hand tightly and said he was pleased to meet me. "And how is Hassanali? I haven't seen him for a while. Is he not coming home to Zanzibar to visit *Mzee* Ebrahim anymore?" he inquired, playing with his black-and-white beard. Dad had also had business dealings with him when he lived in Zanzibar.

He then turned his attention back to me. "How are you doing in school? You were born here, so come and settle on this beautiful island after you finish schooling. We need young educated people."

All I could do was nod in agreement. Royalty are good at small talk!

The room was lavishly decorated with portraits of previous Zanzibari rulers and Arabic ornaments. The lush carpets laid out on the floor looked so expensive that one thought twice before stepping on them.

After some small talk, the sultan and my grandfather had some business to attend to, so they retired in the anteroom. After half an hour they returned, and we were served halva and coffee, in accordance with the traditional Zanzibari custom. I left the palace excited that I had personally met the sultan of Zanzibar—an honour not easily attainable, even to a resident of the island. I bragged about my achievement for days when I returned to school.

My grandfather, Ebrahim, who had two younger brothers, Haji and Karim, had made a fortune in business in Zanzibar. Financed by my grandfather, the three brothers started a partnership in Dar es Salaam in 1926 called Haji Brothers, dealing in silk, ivory, and curios. They also started another business, called the East African Cotton Company.

Both businesses were very successful. My dad and his younger brother, Kassamali, worked with Haji Brothers briefly. The three brothers even donated a building to be used as a girls' school, next to the main *jamatkhana* (Ismaili prayer house) in downtown Dar es Salaam. After a few years, however, my grandfather discovered some inconsistencies in certain business transactions. Much to their dislike, the two younger brothers were asked to explain.

This began an argument that culminated in a fistfight, and my grandfather, the financier of the whole project, was beaten on the forehead and needed hospital treatment. The partnership was dissolved in May 1939, but the repercussions of this family feud lasted for many years. For three generations the split among the Ladha brothers, their children, and grandchildren was such that they stopped speaking to one another. There was absolutely no contact among them. Children were born to their children, and they grew up to be adults without knowing each other.

I vividly remember when I was vice-president of the student union at Dar es Salaam University, and Gulamhussein Haji Ladha's son, a freshman at the university, was having some difficulties. He was directed to see me. We had never met in our lives, and it was only during our conversation that we realized we were first cousins. Small world, as they say!

Haji Brothers flourished into a respectable and leading city business where the rich and famous shopped, including the country's British governor. But the Ladha family never reunited, and when its patriarch, my grandfather, passed away, no one from his brothers' families even attended the funeral in Zanzibar. What a tragic finale for someone who had done everything for his brothers.

My paternal grandmother, a domineering woman, initially bullied my mother, who was timid by nature and temperamentally not very strong. But later, things changed over time. The status quo was not tolerated. The domineering mother-in-law lost her status. Arguments in the family affected the men (my grandfather, father, and uncle) and, in turn, the business—until the time came when my dad, fed up with the family feuds, decided to leave Zanzibar.

One of Dad's Zanzibari friends had gone earlier to Lindi. In fact, quite a few Ismailis from Zanzibar had settled in Lindi, so Dad decided to go there to seek a new life, leaving Mom and their four young children in Zanzibar.

Lindi had a mini Zanzibari community, so it was easy for Dad to adjust. He quickly fit in. He was a hardworking man, but he had never worked for anyone in his life. Miraculously, he had no problem getting a job with Smith McKenzie & Company. After Dad had established himself, we joined him in Lindi. My grandparents came to Lindi to try to persuade Dad to return to Zanzibar and take charge of the business, but, proud that he was, he refused. The Zanzibar enterprise finally collapsed due to a lack of proper direction and leadership. It was a sad finale to what had once been a classical example of a successful and thriving family enterprise built on hard work.

* * *

The pomp and pageantry of the sultanate of Zanzibar came to an abrupt end when the sultan was toppled in a revolution on January 12, 1964. Only a month earlier, on December 10, 1963, Zanzibar had become independent, with an elected government under the Commonwealth, and Sultan Sayyid Jamshid bin Abdullah—who had succeeded his father in July 1963—had become the constitutional monarch.

But on that January day, as Sauti Ya Unguja radio (the Voice of Zanzibar) was playing music, an authoritative male voice came on suddenly: *"Mimi ni field marshal John Okello"* (I am Field Marshal John Okello). He announced that he had staged a coup and taken over the government, overthrown the sultan, and proclaimed Zanzibar a republic.

People could hear gunfire coming from the Ngambu area. The news spread across town that Mau Mau (Kikuyu fighters from Kenya) had landed in Zanzibar with guns. Since the town of Zanzibar had narrow streets and houses close together, neighbours could easily pass information to one another from their windows or balconies and thus throughout the town.

Several hundred armed men, under the leadership of the "field marshal"—a little-known man who had lived on Pemba Island—had descended on Zanzibar to carry out the revolution. The result was a massacre between January 18 and 20, 1964, of some five thousand to twenty thousand Arabs and Asians whose families had been living in Zanzibar for centuries. From a plane and a helicopter, the Italian filmmaker Gualtiero Jacopetti shot the operations as they took place; the resulting shockumentary,

Africa Addio, premiered in 1966 and represents the only existing document of the mass murder.

A widow named Aminabai, a well-known Zanzibar resident who cleaned the *jamatkhana*, was out with her two sons, Ali and Mohamed, when they were confronted by a group of gunmen. One of the men took away Mohamed's shirt and the other took away Ali's bicycle. They were asked to put their hands up in the air and then one of the men suddenly shot Mohamed.

Mohamed lay on the ground, asking for water. Aminabai went berserk, crying and begging for someone to give water to her son. No one had the courage to give him water for fear of being shot themselves. Mohamed lay helplessly on the ground, dying and asking for water as his last wish. One brave woman eventually lowered a container of water from her balcony with a rope, but by that time Mohamed was dead.

Aminabai ran around the street like a mad woman, wailing and crying. Later, one Zanzibar resident, Ashok Mulji, received a telephone call from his uncle saying someone had been shot dead near his house, which was some thousand metres away. It was confirmed later that this was Aminabai's other son, Ali. His body lay in the street for some time, until some Ismailis from the *jamatkhana* came and took it away.

Aminabai lost her senses and never recovered from the loss of her two sons. Ali, the elder one, had told his mother that since he had recently acquired a job, she could take life easy and give up her work at the *jamatkhana*. This dream never came true, though Aminabai had considered cleaning the *jamatkhana* not as a job, but as her *seva* (service) to the imam.

The revolution took the lives of two brothers and left Aminabai to suffer the loss of her sons, who were innocent and had nothing to do with politics. They were at the wrong place at the wrong time. All they had wanted was to give back a little comfort to their mother in her old age. But destiny snatched that away from them.

"I remember Mohamed and Ali used to wait for their mother opposite our house at night while Aminabai was cleaning the *jamatkhana*," Mulji recalled. "The boys would go to sleep on the *baraza* (cement porch) of the *jamatkhana*. Their mother would wake them up and take them home. The lady was just trying to make a living and bring up her sons with whatever she could manage, and tragically her dreams never came true."

Many Ismailis took refuge in the *jamatkhana*, where shelter and food was provided. Fortunately, the revolutionaries respected the sanctity of a religious place and did not attack it, and many Ismailis stayed there until they felt comfortable enough to leave.

Thousands of Arabs fled the island. The Communist-trained "field marshal" John Okello, the mastermind of the revolution, won considerable support from the Africans. Sheikh Abeid Amani Karume, leader of the Afro-Shirazi Party, was installed as the president of the People's Republic of Zanzibar and Pemba; Sheikh Kassam Hanga as prime minister; and Abdulrahman Mohamed Babu, leader of the new left-wing *Umma* (the masses) Party (formed by the defectors from the Zanzibar Nationalist Party), as minister of Defence and External Affairs.

The cabinet and all government departments were placed under the control of the thirty-member Revolutionary Council, which was vested with temporary legislative powers. Zanzibar was proclaimed a one-party state, and the new government, with powers to confiscate any immovable property without compensation except in cases of undue hardship, nationalized all land.

After the revolution, there was fierce political activity among foreign powers. American and British diplomats were kicked out of Zanzibar. East Germany and the Soviet Union quickly established their presence on the island, and Zanzibar became a pawn between the superpowers of the West (the United States) and the East (the USSR). Just days after the revolution, the Soviets came with an offer for military aid while the Americans offered air support through Ethiopia's emperor Haile Selassie.

Tanganyika President Julius Nyerere was afraid. He didn't want the island of Zanzibar, which was at his country's doorstep, to be dominated by communists and become the "Cuba of East Africa." So, he invited President Karume to join with the mainland to form a union, which would come to be known as Tanzania. Karume agreed. As a result, Zanzibar's revolution lasted for less than two months.

Sheikh Karume became the first vice-president of the new union government, and several Zanzibaris, including Sheikh Abdulrahman Mohamed Babu, became ministers in a move to appease the population of the Zanzibar archipelago.

Following university, I became a member of Aga Khan's Dar Provincial Council and was appointed to a three-member delegation charged with facilitating and resettling Zanzibaris on the mainland. Our team would go to the island to interview Ismailis and help them in whatever way we could. During one of these visits, a highly politicized immigration officer wouldn't let me board the flight back to Dar because I was a Zanzibar-born person—he felt it should be my duty to stay and help with the reconstruction of the country. "This is your home. You should be helping the revolution," was his argument.

Another point of contention for him was my profession. My Tanzanian passport stated my profession as a journalist. "You are the guys who are saying that Zanzibar will become the Cuba of East Africa," the officer said. The *Standard* had editorially criticized the Zanzibar revolution and the atrocities that followed.

Even my explanation that I was in Zanzibar not on assignment for the paper but to visit my uncle who lived on the island brought no results. However, to my good fortune, the principal immigration officer interrupted and, after listening to my explanation, escorted me to the plane, minutes before it took off. I quit the delegation and never again went to Zanzibar while I lived in Tanzania.

Zanzibar has an interesting, exciting, and tumultuous but rich history. The islands of Unguja and Pemba, the two main islands that form Zanzibar, had been an Arab sultanate since the nineteenth century. In 1832, the ruler of Oman, Seyyid Said bin Sultan, transferred his capital from Muscat to Zanzibar, becoming the first sultan of Zanzibar. There is ample archaeological and historical evidence to suggest that people of diverse cultural and racial backgrounds visited the islands for hundreds, even thousands, of years, before becoming permanent residents. A lot of racial intermingling occurred among the populations to produce the present-day social fabric, commonly known as the cultural potpourri—an identity that provides a source of pride for Zanzibar's residents. For centuries Zanzibar has not only had its own glorious history, but has radiated its cultural, political, and financial influence to countries beyond its shores.

Several Asian businessmen rose to prominence in Zanzibar and other areas of East Africa: Zanzibar had Tharia Topan; Mombasa, Kenya, had Allidina Visram; and Uganda had the Madhvani family. These pioneers laid foundations for their communities in East Africa.

A Student in Dar

AFRICANS, ASIANS, AND WHITES LIVED SEPARATELY IN Tanganyika, each race in its own residential areas, learning in separate schools and socializing in separate clubs. They hardly ever intermingled, except at the employer-employee level. I had no relationship with Africans outside the master-servant dichotomy. In keeping with the colonial setup, everyone had African servants; that was how race relations worked in colonial Africa.

After I finished my Senior Cambridge, or Grade 12, in Lindi, I went to Dar es Salaam in 1961 for a Higher School Certificate (HSC), which was a two-year prerequisite course for university entrance. It was here that I met Africans on an equal level for the first time. Prior to this, I had studied in schools where all students were Asians.

Our class of approximately twenty-five, however, included only one African—who happened to be the brother of Tanzania's then finance minister, Paul Bomani—though there were lots of African students in other classes. Francis was tall, handsome, and friendly, and we soon became good friends. I didn't see anything different in him and lamented the fact that I hadn't had the opportunity to meet him earlier. Unfortunately, our friendship was cut short. He was awarded a U.S. scholarship, presumably through his brother's connections, and went to study in the United States.

Since my parents were still in Lindi, I lived as a boarder in Upanga, an Asian area in Dar es Salaam, with a young Ismaili couple. I shared a room with another boarder, Zul, who was from Mtwara. We would study till late during exams, our books spread on the dining table. However, our landlady didn't appreciate the lights being on late at night. After a few days, we noticed that the bulbs above the dining table were missing. We got the message. She cared more about her power bill than about our education.

A few students from the neighbourhood went at night to study at our school, which was within walking distance. Schools were kept open in the evenings during exams for students wishing to study, and we would gather there until our final exams were over.

Our group was only the second batch of HSC students, as the program had been introduced a year prior to our arrival. The HSC was the only coeducational class in an all-boys school, so we were the envy of all the students. In my class, we had only five boys among probably four times the number of girls. I was quite popular with the girls with my pranks and mischievous nature. All HSC male students were made prefects, so we had to wear a blue tie, a white shirt, and grey shorts.

The University of Dar es Salaam (UDSM) was first established in 1961 as a college of the University of London. It became a constituent college of the University of East Africa in 1963 and an independent national university in 1970, along with the other constituent colleges of Nairobi (Kenya) and Makerere (Uganda).

I was privileged to be among the first students of this new campus when in 1964 the university was moved to its own magnificent buildings on Observation Hill, sixteen kilometres northwest of the city centre. Each student had a room on the campus, and when we arrived, the newly painted rooms smelled of freshness. Although the new campus was located several miles out of town, in an area called Ubongo, it was served well by an excellent bus service. In a country with a largely illiterate population, university students were considered the privileged class.

For most students, the university provided the first opportunity for the three races to study together as equals. The majority of students in the university were Africans, followed by Asians and then a few whites, mainly from the United States or European countries. The local white families had chosen to educate their children in England, perhaps thinking that local education was not good enough. Whatever the reason, they were noticeably absent.

I was particularly pleased to have the opportunity to forge friendships with Africans, since in my previous schools I hadn't had even the chance to meet them. I considered this to be my first and last chance. But to my disappointment, other Asian students didn't see it that way. I was horrified to note that, with few exceptions, the Asian mentality of clinging together in clusters of their own during meals continued at the university. Very little effort was made to mingle with African students, giving the impression to the majority of the future leaders of Africa that the Asians were too proud to associate with them—that what they had heard about the Asians being selfish exploiters was true.

The so-called Asian intellectuals didn't realize that they were in university as representatives of their communities and that the onus was on them to turn the tables. Here was an ideal opportunity for them to build bridges with the Africans and to act as ambassadors for their communities, but they let the opportunity go. They were more interested in dating girls and taking them to the Friday cinema than facing this important task.

Because I mingled with the Africans, I was considered an ideal candidate for office in the students' union. Several African students approached me to run. After careful consideration, I decided to plunge in and sought office as second vice-president of the Tanzanian Students' Union. Candidates were given two weeks to campaign, and I went around the campus meeting students and familiarizing them with my policies. Two days before elections a candidates' forum was held, where we presented our platforms and answered questions from the audience.

I woke up early on election day. When the results were announced, to my amazement I was elected as the only non-African member of the executive. I was the talk of the campus. Tanzania at the time had two vice-presidents—First Vice-President Abeid Karume, who was also president of Zanzibar, and Second Vice-President Rashidi Kawawa. In jest, my friends started calling me the third vice-president.

While at Dar University, I also became friends with an African student named David. As mentioned earlier, this was the first time I had met an African on equal footing. We became friends because we had similar interests; we could talk about things openly, without any reservations. David was in my political science class. I sat beside him in the lecture theatre and we started chatting. He was a Chagga by tribe and a coffee farmer's son from northern Tanzania. This was his first time in the capital city, so everything was new to him. He invited me for beer at the students' union bar one evening. We became *rafiki* (friends), and I promised to show him the city since I owned a car and Dar was also my hometown.

It was due to my upbringing and nature that I became friends with people very easily. I actually got this ability from my father, who, as a plantation owner, had lived among Africans and Arabs in Zanzibar. I lament the fact that as a student my early education was limited to South Asian schools, which prevented me from making friends with Africans at an early age—but even as kid, I mingled with our servants at home quite easily. Many times I would eat with one servant because I loved his staple food, *ugali*—made from maize flour and usually eaten with fish or meat on top. To this day, I love to eat *ugali na samaki* (maize-flour meal with fish), which is available in some Canadian cities in restaurants owned by East African Asians and has become a popular dish among Asians.

Since my initial contact with Africans was at the servant level, I had decided to make a real effort to nurture and cement my friendship with David to the fullest extent. As promised, one weekend I took David to the city for an introductory familiarization drive. He enjoyed the drive along Independence Avenue, Market Street, Kariakoo Market, the Mnazi Mmoja grounds, St. Joseph's Cathedral, the main Ismaili *jamatkhana*, the Upanga area, Oyster Bay, and other landmarks of the city. I showed him African as well as Asian and European areas of Dar.

The highlight of the drive was when we stopped for snacks at Naaz Restaurant, a popular restaurant frequented by Ismailis. We had kebabs and samosas. David found the delicacies delicious, but too spicy. However, he enjoyed them to the fullest—along with gallons of water and Coke.

So our friendship blossomed to the extent that David became a frequent visitor at my parents' home when I visited them on weekends. He accompanied me there for Sunday meals a few times as well. He really enjoyed talking to Dad in authentic Zanzibari Swahili. As friends, we could openly discuss sensitive issues such as race relations without any problems—issues that we would not dare discuss in public with others.

As an example, one day I asked him, "Why do Africans hate Asians so much?" and by the same token he wanted to know, "Why do Asians exploit Africans?" These were taboo topics—embarrassing, sensitive, and controversial if discussed in public.

"Asians do not basically exploit Africans as such," I explained. "First of all, you have to realize that since most Asians are shopkeepers and businessmen, they are involved in an economic exercise based on profit making, which Africans perceive as exploitation. Profit making can be construed as exploitation, but that's the nature of the business."

David explained that most Africans, feeling that the Asians' sole motive was to exploit Africans by overcharging them, hated Asians. However, after meeting so many Asian students in the university, David said he realized that they were considerate and friendly. "But you are totally different, there's no question about it," he said, smiling broadly. I was flattered by the compliment.

"But, David, don't forget you have come in contact with me not at a shopkeeper-customer level, but on a student-to-student and friend-to-friend basis. Our relationship has been on equal footing, which is most important. You are the first African I have had as a friend. I have liked you and you have liked me, and I hope our friendship continues throughout our lives."

Although David didn't appear to be quite satisfied with my explanation, he didn't argue.

"More and more people will experience what we have experienced, and more and more friendships will be built, breaking the racial barrier and dissolving the racial hatred between Asians and Africans in this country in years to come," I continued. "That is bound to happen. A beginning will be made in elementary schools, secondary schools, and universities till people reach adulthood."

David listened to me attentively and without interrupting. When I finished, he stood up and all of a sudden came towards me and hugged me. "Yes, *mahatma* (saint), yes. I hope your predictions are right. Let's go, I'll buy you a beer." And off we went to the students' union bar.

One day, I found David quite distraught. I could tell from just looking at his long face. "David, what's the matter? Please tell me," I insisted.

He said he had asked an Asian girl out to next Saturday's dance, and she'd turned him down, saying she had a boyfriend. He didn't believe her and felt that she had turned him down because he was black. "It's purely racial. Your Asian girls would never go out with Africans. That's it," he said. "Would you allow your sister to go out with me?" Before I could answer, he kept speaking. "Then why would anyone who doesn't even know me go out with me? All you Asians are the same. Bloody racists." He banged the desk as he spoke.

I couldn't believe what he was saying. He was very upset and angry. I had never seen him like this. I felt I had to calm him down and put the record straight.

"David, my dear friend. First of all, you do not go to just any girl and ask her to go out, irrespective of whether she is Asian or African. Even I wouldn't do it. Maybe the girl has a boyfriend. You have to know the girl before you ask her out. That's pure common sense."

"But the girl is in my English class, and we see each other practically every day," David responded.

"You are also personalizing the discussion by bringing my sister into it," I said. "As it turns out, of my two sisters, one is studying in the U.S. and is already married. The other is engaged to be married, so the issue doesn't arise, but even if she were available, it would not be up to me to ask her to go out with you or anyone else. It would be up to her. If she meets a boy and likes him and wants to go out, then it's her decision. That's the way our family functions. We don't order our sisters to date someone, and most Asian families these days operate that way. The days of forced marriages may be taking place in India or in some Asian communities, but not in our Ismaili community."

David looked straight at me, listening to my explanation as I continued. "This brings me to our original discussion the other day—contact between people, between different races, which is going to break the racial barrier. This has been lacking so far, and for most people university is their first contact with members of different races. As I said, give it time and you will see that it will come eventually. But don't be distraught because one girl has refused to go out with you. I have also been refused dates by Asian girls and, if you must know, by an Asian girl who knows me and doesn't even have a boyfriend. You think I am going to sit here and brood or agonize over it? No way, my friend. Life has to go on. There are many fish in the sea, as they say, and better ones, too."

Though I lectured David on race relations, I often wondered about the future of Asian-African relations at the university and its repercussions in the future—which I felt wasn't very bright judging from the way things were progressing on campus between the two races. Most Asian and African students, I noticed, went around in groups and sat in those same groups at meals, talking in their own languages, ignoring others sitting around the table. African students were equally guilty of sitting in their own tribal groups and talking in the Chagga, Makonde, or Masai language, being insensitive to other students around them. None of them had the urge to build bridges with each other.

No group was making an effort to build friendships. On social evenings, groups of Asians and groups of Africans came on campus for movie nights or dances with their girlfriends or dates, while others, who were in the mostly dateless majority, watched with envy as the dance floor was patronized by the lucky few.

Only a few Asian students who cared about interracial relations made genuine attempts to build lasting friendships with African students during their university years. Most students, Asian and African, appeared to have one mission only: to get their degrees and get out of university as soon as possible. It was unfortunate that university was not seen as a place to build friendships and foster interracial harmony—this goal was just not on most students' radar screens.

One other African who became a good friend of mine while at university was Joseph Warioba, a tall, skinny student who was one of those who had encouraged me to run for office with the students' union. He was a senior and ahead of me by a year, studying law. While visiting Calgary some decades later, I saw the Tanzanian newspaper the *Daily News*, and on the front page was a picture of Joseph with some other people. The caption under the picture said, in bold type, that Joseph Warioba, Tanzania's prime minister, was attending this particular function somewhere in the country.

What a surprise it was for me to learn that my dear friend had attained the highest office in the land by becoming the prime minister of the country! What an achievement and an honour. I was proud of him. On the way back to Edmonton, I told my wife about our university days together and how we had worked jointly in organizing the student union. After about a week's time, I told my wife that I must phone Joseph in Tanzania to congratulate him.

My wife politely reminded me that he was prime minister of the country and that it may not be so easy to phone him. I agreed, but the worst that could happen is that his office would refuse to accept a call from an ordinary Joe Blow in Canada. No harm would be done—I would swallow the insult and mention the incident to no one. So I plucked up the courage and phoned the international operator in Montreal, and I asked her to put me through to the State House in Dar es Salaam, Tanzania.

"Sir, is it a residence or business?" I was asked.

"No, I want the government house in Dar es Salaam, Tanzania."

Then I heard the Canadian operator telling her Tanzanian counterpart, "Ma'am, we want the government house in Dar es Salaam, Tanzania."

Learning this, the Tanzanian operator was flabbergasted; she told the person next to her, in Swahili, "Looks like this person wants to speak to the prime minister at the State House." Now she had a question for the Canadian operator: "Who is calling?"

The Canadian operator asked me, "Sir, who is calling?"

Trying to keep my identity secret, I replied, "Tell them it's his friend from Canada."

"Ma'am, it's his friend from Canada." The two operators probably thought it was his friend the prime minister of Canada calling. (Brian Mulroney was the prime minister at the time.)

There was silence for a split second and suddenly a voice came on, saying, "State House, Dar es Salaam." The Canadian operator repeated the request of the call, and after a brief moment, another voice came on the line: "Joseph Warioba speaking!"

"Joseph! It's Mansoor Ladha, calling from Canada!"

"Hello, Ladha, how are you? Good to hear from you. It's been a long time since we talked or met. What have you been up to? When are you coming here, my friend?"

I was flattered that he still remembered me and still considered me as a friend.

"Hopefully soon, while you are still the PM. But I would want you to assure me that when I come, you will be at the airport to receive me, with outriders on motorbikes and you in your official car with a Tanzanian flag in front."

"You've got it, my friend. Just let me know when you're coming and I'll be there at the airport to receive you. That's a promise."

"I was expecting you in Vancouver during the recent Commonwealth heads summit [in 1987]," I said, "but I noticed you were absent. If you had come, I would have come to Vancouver to meet you."

"Yes, I didn't come because the president went, and when the president is away, I have to be inside the country. That's how it works."

"So how are things in Tanzania otherwise?"

"Same old problems," he replied. "We have the same old problems of economic growth and development. We are gradually trying to overcome them."

"Well, Joseph, thanks for taking my call. I don't want to take too much of your time. I just called to congratulate you on becoming the PM and to let you know that I was proud to learn about it. It was a pleasure talking to you, and I will definitely surprise you one of these days with a visit. Hang in there, my friend. Goodbye and best of luck in all your endeavours."

"Thanks for calling and *kwaheri* [goodbye], Ladha!"

Unfortunately, I couldn't go to Tanzania while he was still prime minister, so I never got to sit in a car with a Tanzanian flag fluttering on it and several outriders ahead of the entourage. My bad luck and my loss.

Joseph served as prime minister of Tanzania from 1985 to 1990. From 1976 to 1983, he had been the attorney general and, later, minister of justice. Prior to that, in 1966, President Ben Mkapa had appointed Joseph as chairman of the Presidential Commission against Government Corruption; in 2007 he was chosen to lead a Commonwealth observer group on Nigerian elections.

His most recent endeavour was as chairman of the thirty-member Constitutional Review Commission tasked with studying and making recommendations on the future constitution of Tanzania. Unfortunately, during my visit to Tanzania in 2015, Joseph was in Burundi on official business and we couldn't meet.

Changing Times

"*BWANA, BWANA, UHURU, UHURU!*" (SIR, SIR, FREEDOM, Freedom!)

"I just heard it—that the country is going to be independent." Puffing and panting, Juma came into the living room, back from the market after buying the day's vegetables.

I closed my book and rose from the armchair. "What nonsense are you talking?" I said, having no clue of the situation at hand.

"The country is going to be independent soon, and there is going to be a black government in the country, replacing all the *mzungus* (white guys)," he said proudly.

Africans replacing white men? We thought old man Juma had gone crazy. It was unthinkable. Now Juma, who had been with my family for many years, could be trusted as a faithful Muslim. He prayed at least three times a day in between his chores, and there was no question he would be saying the truth. However, I decided to double-check the story. I went to the popular Palm Beach Hotel in search of someone who could verify it. The hotel was the favoured watering hole of politicians, government officials, and civil servants wanting a drink after work. It was the place where you could always pick up local gossip and rumours of what was going on in the government. I met Amir Jamal, a leading member of the Asian community who was very active in national politics, seated with his African colleagues, having a few drinks and obviously discussing the forthcoming events. Amir, considered a staunch nationalist, was one of the Asians who had taken an active part in the fight to end colonialism. He was one of those who had sided with Nyerere from the beginning.

The group appeared to be unusually jubilant. Although I was an eighteen-year-old high school student, Amir knew me and my family. I took Amir aside and asked him what was going on.

"So you have also heard about it! Nothing stays secret in this country for too long. It's a rumour mill." He smiled. "However, keep it to yourself. All I can tell you is to continue reading newspapers. Don't worry—it will be public knowledge soon." That told me everything I wanted to know. I thanked him and left.

The following week, newspapers ran banner headlines: "Independence here!" read one; "Freedom at last!" declared another; "We are going to be free," blared a third. Print media and radio had a field day, with commentaries tracing the country's history from colonialism to independence. Tanganyika—the Swahili name means "sail in the wilderness"—had been under British colonial rule since the First World War.

The British Colonial Office then released more details. It was established that the country would be independent on December 9, 1961. There was to be a black African government. White government ministers and top civil servants were to be replaced. The Africans were jubilant.

As a prelude to independence, businesses were periodically broken into and goods stolen in our neighbourhood. As independence drew closer, so did the necessity of measures for safety and security. My father hired a night watchman, and we also kept a German shepherd. Whether we could trust the watchman was another question: there were instances where watchmen had either disappeared after a break-in or joined forces with the thieves. Fortunately, during the transitional period nothing eventful happened to us, and we embraced the independence period with joy as citizens of a newly emergent state with high expectations.

After I left Dar University in 1966, I came in contact with young Ismaili professionals. The group consisted of recent graduates of different specialties, who had come forward as volunteers to serve the Ismaili community. Volunteerism is one of the pillars of our faith, and the Ismaili establishment was keen to harness youthful energies in the right direction. This was the beginning of the Organization of Youth Co-ordination (OYC) under the Aga Khan Provincial Council. I was appointed vice chairman of the group, and Firoz Karim, a senior economist with the National Development Corporation who now resides in Victoria, British Columbia, was appointed chairman.

The OYC organized several functions focussing on youths. One of the highlights was a national conference on the role of youths in Tanzania, at which the then minister of finance, Amir Jamal, was the keynote speaker. Jamal, who held many high posts in Tanzania including that of finance minister, later served as Tanzanian ambassador to the United Nations in Geneva. He died in Vancouver in 1995 after years of debilitating illness, which he had fought with fortitude. Born in Tanzania, Jamal came from a trading family. He fully participated in the nationalist movement. He continued to serve the country after independence, regularly being appointed a minister from 1961 until 1989—often appointed to ministries requiring strong management and selfless commitment. Jamal's utter integrity, dedication, selfless service, and great ability and personal goodness were recognized throughout Tanzania. He was repeatedly elected with ever-increasing majorities from predominantly African constituencies.

The conference was a great success, boosting the image of the OYC. Later, Karim was appointed as a member of the Aga Khan Provincial Council, and I became chair of the OYC. In a few months, I was appointed a member of the Aga Khan Provincial Council. Both of our appointments were considered to be historic because this was perhaps the first time that young adults were appointed to the Aga Khan council, presumably to bring in new, progressive, and fresh ideas. We made quite an impact in council debates and during discussions, such that even the seasoned members of the council were swayed and saw issues in a way they had never seen before.

My involvement with the OYC and later the Aga Khan council provided me with excellent experience in dealing with the public. Members of the community believe that whoever has served the Ismaili community will have no problem serving in any other capacity outside the community. Community members are hard nuts to crack, and they are known for hassling their leaders. If you can handle Ismailis, the belief goes, you can handle anyone.

I met my wife in 1966, but like every young man I found the road to love a little rocky. When I was a high school student, I fell for a pretty girl who was a year behind me. I was shy and I hid my feelings towards her. I never got a chance to declare them openly before I had to leave Lindi for Dar es Salaam, and we lost touch forever.

While I was in my second year of HSC, I became friendly with a girl who attended the school. She had a wonderful smile and charming personality and was good-looking. I was very popular among the girls, but speechless when I faced this girl. I had several chances to express my feelings but somehow feared rejection, though I had every indication that she also liked me.

I took this crush on her to university, where our friendship continued. We went on several dates. After university she was posted to a town in northern Tanzania, and she continued writing to me. A few years later she suddenly stopped writing, and I heard she had got married without even telling me she had switched her affection. Jilted and distraught, I felt like a piece of discarded furniture. But later I learned that one can chalk things like this up to a form of experience and the bumpy road to love.

I met the married couple several years later at a wedding reception in Vancouver. They were sitting at a table with a friend and his wife. I stopped by to say hello to my friend when all of a sudden, this woman stands up and says, "I hope you remember me."

"I am sorry, I don't," I said looking at her straight in the eye.

"How can you forget? You used to date me in university!"

I was taken aback. How silly of me to not recognize the girl I had dated. I was embarrassed. She looked different. I apologized for not recognizing her and kissed her on both cheeks.

During my involvement in the community, I came in contact with Anaar Tejpar, who was the OYC secretary. She was also LR—London Returned. In Africa, it was common for colonial subjects to go to London, England, for further education. Upon their return they were called LR, signifying high achievement and prestige. Anaar was lively and bubbly, and she joked a lot. Her outspokenness and frank ideas really impressed me, and we became good friends. The two of us instantly connected, sharing laughter and time together. We "hung out" as friends before our relationship blossomed into a full-blown romance. On September 14, 1967, we were married.

Indian weddings are elaborate, expensive ventures, some going on for a week of festivities. We planned our wedding to last four days, including pre- and post-wedding ceremonies and a banquet to be attended by office colleagues, friends, relatives, and immediate family members. We had a long list of colleagues to invite, from both the *Standard* and my wife's office at the Ford Foundation.

The Aga Khan council at the time had decreed that guests at weddings should not exceed 250, as an austerity measure to cut down expenses. My wife's uncle, Abdallah Tejpar, was president of Aga Khan Territorial Council at the time, which placed an added burden on the family to stick to the regulation and set an example for others. However, having reviewed the guest list, we couldn't omit anyone, and the number of guests totalled close to five hundred. As guilty parties, a representative each from the bride's and groom's sides were summoned by the council and penalized accordingly.

Our married life was happy and both of us had excellent jobs. I was with the *Standard* newspaper; she was secretary to the head of the Ford Foundation in Tanzania and later with the American embassy. With our well-placed jobs, we became social butterflies, attending various embassy and government functions.

Our life changed as soon as we entered parenthood with the birth of our son, Hanif, on November 24, 1970. My father, who named him, was particularly pleased at his birth, and there was happiness all around the Ladha family as our bundle of joy was the first born to the eldest child of the family.

Watching my dad turn into a granddad was exciting. It was a pleasure watching him play with my son when Hanif turned two. Dad's eyes would light up when his grandson came running into his arms. The most satisfying thing for me was when my father heard Hanif call him "Grandpa." When Hanif was older, my father would proudly take him to his shop, introducing him to his customers.

Dad's store in Dar es Salaam, called Hassanali Produce Store, was located right in front of Dar's famous Kariakoo Market. The store sold wholesale products such as flour, onions, potatoes, rice, soap, and cooking oil to retail merchants and small businesses. Kariakoo Market, today one of the city's tourist attractions, was and remains the largest market of its kind in East Africa.

As the city centre's most African district, Kariakoo was left to the African population after the First World War. The area hence combines both tribal and religious identities of the country, resulting in one of the most fascinating and colourful markets on the continent.

Today, every tourist to Tanzania visits Kariakoo Market to get a feel for the African market environment—a taste of African life—and perhaps to buy something. Everything can be found at Kariakoo Market. It's a place where you can find locals haggling over the price of freshly caught fish, or have your chicken slaughtered the Muslim way (halal) and cleaned while you wait. I remember seeing Asian women pressing the stomachs of live chickens before buying them, to ensure that each bird had enough meat to feed their families. I also remember my mother taking eggs in her hands and holding them up to the sunlight to check for any impurities in them. I could never authoritatively determine if she was right or wrong.

In the market today, one can find vegetable vendors, fruit stalls, freshly cooked meats, aromatic spices, herbs, coffee, handicrafts, textiles, local brews (*pombe*), and children's toys made from wire and recycled tin cans. Old men sell medicinal herbs, lotions, and powders in little bottles salvaged from hospitals. Farmers from all over bring their products to sell.

People may enjoy the hustle and bustle of the daily rituals at Kariakoo Market, but they would be well advised to leave their valuables at home. This giant supermarket is well known for thieves and pickpockets who prey on innocent tourists. The market is so overcrowded that one has little more than elbowroom to move—an ideal setting for light-fingered thieves.

Independence

We, the people of Tanganyika, would like to light a candle and put it on top of Mount Kilimanjaro which would shine beyond our borders giving hope where there was despair, love where there was hate, and dignity where before there was only humiliation. We cannot, unlike other countries, send rockets to the moon. But we can send rockets of love and hope to all our fellow [humans] wherever they may be.

—JULIUS KAMBARAGE NYERERE, STATEMENT IN TANGANYIKA'S LEGISLATIVE ASSEMBLY, OCTOBER 1959

A NATIVE OF BUTIAMA, ON THE EASTERN SHORE OF LAKE Victoria, Julius Nyerere was born around 1923, one of twenty-six children of the aristocratic but illiterate chief of the Zanaki tribe, Nyerere Burito, who had several wives.

Julius Nyerere had practically no contact with modern civilization until he was twelve because, as a boy, he herded sheep and led a typical tribal life. His life changed completely after attending a Roman Catholic mission school at Tabora, in Central Province. He was baptized as a Roman Catholic when he was twenty. He entered Makerere University in Kampala, Uganda, in 1943 and became the first Tanganyikan to study at a British university when he went to the University of Edinburgh on a government scholarship in 1949. On returning to Tanganyika in October 1952, after obtaining a master's degree in history and economics, he became a teacher at the St. Francis School in Pugu, near Dar es Salaam.

Nyerere renewed ties with the Tanganyika African Association and was elected its president in 1953; then on July 7, 1954, he transformed the organization into the Tanganyika African National Union (TANU), a political party aimed at obtaining independence from Britain. The party's constitution stressed peace, equality, and racial harmony, while opposing tribalism, isolationism, and discrimination. Nyerere was to become the first African prime minister of independent Tanganyika. Not only the African majority but also the Asian and European minorities placed their hopes and aspirations on the shoulders of this man, hoping he would prove wrong all those critics who had predicted chaos when African government took over. Asians had heard about the Edinburgh-educated teacher. They hoped that he, as someone with Western education, would be reasonable—more sympathetic to minorities. They were told he was a learned man and that he was in favour of a multiracial country in which every race was welcome. These were soothing words and encouraging to non-Africans. Asians in the business community were restless because they didn't know what to expect. Many of them were of the third generation born in Tanganyika and knew of no other place to live.

Changes were also gradually taking place in neighbouring Kenya, where the Mau Mau—Kikuyu freedom fighters led by Jomo Kenyatta—scared the hell out of everybody, mostly the whites and the Asians. Kenyatta went on to become the first president of independent Kenya; a British governor of the country dubbed him "the leader of death and darkness." The Mau Mau focussed largely on the whites, who in turn grew increasingly worried about their comfortable, easy life that was crumbling before their eyes. The Mau Mau were mainly fighting for independence in Kenya, and to make their point, they killed a few white farmers living in the so-called White Highlands. Some of the progressive whites blamed themselves, knowing that they had destroyed the old African ways. As colonial rulers, the whites forgot that they were dealing with people—with human beings who had emotions. They didn't acknowledge that they had failed in Africa and had never cared about the plight of the poor African or his future.

When Tanganyika's Independence Day finally arrived, it was a national holiday. Schools, businesses, public buildings, and offices were closed. Shops and businesses were decorated, and streets were lit in the evening with coloured lights. Frightened Asians especially made a great effort to beautify and decorate their shops, businesses, and even dwellings. Asians had to make a show of public support, whether they supported the changing landscape or not. Everyone came out dressed in his or her best attire for the occasion. Children were given miniature flags—both British and the new Tanganyikan flags—as they lined the streets to cheer the dignitaries on their way to the independence ceremony.

Over eighty thousand people gathered at the open-air Dar es Salaam National Stadium to witness the proceedings. At one minute to midnight, the British Union Jack was lowered for the last time. The stadium was plunged into darkness, and as soon as the floodlights came on, the new Tanganyika anthem, "*Mungu ibariki Tanganyika*" (God bless Tanganyika), was played, while the green, black, and orange flag of the new nation was raised. People clapped with jubilation and shouted, "*Uhuru! Uhuru!*"

(Freedom! Freedom!) and "*Uhuru ni kazi! Uhuru ni kazi!*" (Freedom means work!)

Royal Air Force jets roared above in the skies, marking the highlight of the ceremony as Prime Minister Julius Nyerere received the instruments of Tanganyika's independence from Prince Philip, the Duke of Edinburgh. The loudest ovation was reserved for Nyerere—who by now was fondly called *Mwalimu* (teacher)—as he drove around the arena in his open car.

Prime Minister Nyerere, neatly dressed in his dark suit and looking smart, acknowledged the clapping and shouts from the crowd. Addressing the gathering, he said, "Joyful though this moment is, you, sir [speaking to the Duke], have rightly reminded us that it is a moment heavy with responsibility. This our people will appreciate. Our responsibilities towards our own people will, in all conscience, be difficult enough to discharge. In a country such as ours, the struggle to raise the standards of our people and to lift up our economy will be severe; but however severe it may be, it will be waged with all the confidence and resolve that inspire this new nation."

Whenever he stopped to take a breath, the crowd cheered, waving the Tanganyikan flag or calling his name: "Nyerere! Nyerere!"

The new prime minister continued: "In addition, we have wider duties than those we bear towards ourselves alone. We have our responsibilities towards all those other African states with which our links are bound to be so close; and further, even the newest of nations has, in these days, duties towards all the nations upon earth and opportunities to influence by example the policies even of the most powerful."

He told his countrymen to remember this day—Uhuru Day—in their hearts forever. He told them that they should tell their children and grandchildren of its meaning and what it meant to fight for independence.

"Remember, it has been a long, hard struggle to achieve this freedom. Tell your children, the road to freedom has not been easy," he said amid thunderous applause.

"*Uhuru! Uhuru wananchi!*" (Freedom! Independence, compatriots!) said the headline on the front page of *Uhuru*, the leading Swahili newspaper, the next day. "*Leo ni siku ya furaha sana!*" (Today is a day of great rejoicing!) began the article that followed. "It is a totally special day in the life of every African alive. Today is the day, which is pleasing both for the living and the dead. Today is the greatest, most important holiday. It is a holiday to celebrate our independence."

When Tanganyika became independent, Nyerere, as a devout Pan-Africanist, firmly believed that no country in Africa was free until other, neighbouring African countries were also independent. Hence, he gave strong support to liberation movements such as the Zimbabwe African National Union, the Zimbabwe African People's Union, the African National Congress, the Pan-African Congress of South Africa, the Popular Movement for the Liberation of Angola, the South West Africa's People Organization, and the Front for the Liberation of Mozambique (Frelimo). All these liberation movements operated actively from Dar es Salaam, and Frelimo had used Tanzania as its military and political base from 1964. Tanganyika also became the headquarters of the Organisation of the African Unity liberation committee. All of a sudden, Dar was full of bearded freedom fighters from several African countries, sporting coloured *kitenge* (cotton cloth with various brightly coloured prints) shirts. It was generally believed that Tanzania under Nyerere paid sums well beyond the country's publicized contributions to the liberation movements fighting colonialism.

This financial support met with local resistance and unhappiness, as some citizens felt that Tanganyika would be flooded with refugees from various countries and its economy would not be able to withstand the expenses of hosting these liberation movements. "Is Nyerere trying to bankrupt the country?" "How can we afford to house and feed all these refugees?" These were questions being asked at the time.

Tanganyika became the crossroads of Africa in the heady days of the 1960s through to the somewhat calmer 1980s. Almost everyone who was anyone visited Dar es Salaam, the mecca of Pan-Africanism, during those years to meet Nyerere and the leaders of southern Africa's liberation movements. The Chinese premier Zhou Enlai spoke in 1964 of Africa being "ripe for revolution." Others who came included such dignitaries as Marshal Tito, Olof Palme, Robert F. Kennedy, Henry Kissinger, Che Guevara, and Malcolm X, and sporting legends such as Arthur Ashe. From Africa came leaders including President Gamal Nasser of Egypt, Emperor Haile Selassie of Ethiopia, President William Tubman of Liberia, and a host of others. As one of my colleagues told me, it was an intoxicating time for Africa, and Tanganyika under Nyerere was caught in the middle. Western leftist intellectuals were treating Africa as a test case without knowing much about African realities; they saw Tanzania as some sort of political laboratory as they listened to Mwalimu's great treatises on African socialism and one-party democracy.

Tanganyika didn't have freedom fighters like the Frelimo in Mozambique or the Mau Mau in Kenya; instead, Tanganyika had staunch and devout nationalists like Julius Nyerere, who fought for independence from British colonial rule.

Tanganyika was the first of the initial three East African countries to become independent. Members of the Asian community were given a choice by the departing British: either retain British status or become citizens of the newly independent state. Many Asians suffered from what can be described as a split nationality disorder. Many felt caught between two vibrant cultures: African and Asian. Which way to turn was a dilemma. It was decision time for Asians in Tanganyika.

I remember my father telling the family that our spiritual leader, the Aga Khan, had advised the Ismailis to become citizens of Tanganyika, the country of their birth and of their adoption. So we did not have a choice—the Aga Khan's *farman* (edict) was a command to Ismaili followers. "We must become local citizens," my father emphasized. Hence, 99.9 percent of the local Ismailis became citizens of Tanganyika. Other Asians also became Tanganyikans, while some opted to relocate to Britain or India/Pakistan. Our whole family, all seven of us, took out local citizenship and swore allegiance to Tanganyika. Ismailis are loyal folk. Those who stayed became local citizens, called Tanganyika their homeland, and hoped to remain there for the rest of their lives.

But independence did not bring about the immediate benefits the Africans had anticipated. Despite all the rhetoric and promises from politicians, Tanganyikans saw that their lives hadn't changed in the first couple of years after the country had become independent. A minority of Africans were seen driving Mercedes Benzes and living in big houses in exclusive white areas, while the majority still had to work hard to make a living. "Where are the fruits of independence?" many of them began to ask.

A cab driver named Ramzani explained it to me. "People are growing impatient with the government because they expected miracles and quick-fix benefits when independence came," he said. "They expected these changes overnight. People expected to live in new homes as soon as independence came, but those houses have not even been built yet." The fruits of independence were hard to come by.

Living in independent Africa could be nerve-racking, especially for those belonging to a minority business community, like the Asians. At every stage they encountered so-called authority demanding to inspect their premises or businesses—measures that could clearly be identified as harassment. Following independence, tension in the air was constant among the Asians. The tables were now turned: Africans had become superior over all other races in the country. Those Europeans and Asians who had been in Tanganyika for generations, and who held Tanganyikan passports, were restless and nervous because a minor complaint from a disgruntled political worker or TANU official could have a "foreigner" (regardless of citizenship) thrown out of the country—deported immediately and forever.

The African bureaucrats and civil servants suddenly found themselves with power and limitless authority. This bred corruption. If an Asian's car had a defective signal light, the traffic cop expected to receive a bribe if the driver wanted to avoid prosecution, especially in smaller centres where police were stricter. Labour officials would make sporadic checks on Asian businesses and demand to see labour records. Illiterate Asian shopkeepers, usually very scared of authoritative officialdom, would succumb to bribery demands. And so the spiral would continue. Corruption had taken root from senior bureaucrats and politicians to lower-level civil servants. Front-desk clerks wouldn't bring your files or get your birth certificate or land title documents unless you greased their palms.

At every step of the way, it appeared that the Africans harassed the Asians. Whether Asians went to get a business licence or a car licence or a passport, the clerk sitting behind the counter would deliberately delay providing their document until such time that the Asian applicant, in desperation, was forced to offer what became widely known as *pesa ya chai* (money for tea). It became a ritual; the Asians started to recognize that the Africans wouldn't do their work unless they were offered this "tea money." For the Asians, offering bribes became an automatic thing, while Africans and whites got their business done without any problems. Sometimes, Asians would place extra money in a file in addition to the license fees, to appease the civil servant and expedite the matter and avoid wasting time. These are classic examples of what brown persons faced in a black society—almost every day.

An acquaintance had a shop in a small town called Tukuyu, on the Tanganyika-Malawi border, selling salt, shirts, sugar, and other goods to African small businesses. There was a shortage of bath soap and Colgate toothpaste in the country at one time, so people used to smuggle these items from Malawi and sell them to residents in Tukuyu. This shopkeeper had bought ten bars of bath soap and ten tubes of Colgate and hidden them in his shop. As it turned out, two policemen came to inspect his shop without a warrant, and one dared not pose questions to officials in authority. The shopkeeper allowed them to inspect his shop to their satisfaction. They didn't find anything wrong, except those bars of soap and tubes of toothpaste.

The merchant truthfully pointed out that the merchandise had come from Malawi, and everyone in town was buying them. For hygienic reasons, people have to take a bath and brush their teeth, he explained. The policemen were not satisfied. The shopkeeper was taken to the station and remanded in custody. It was his good fortune that the chief of police, whom he knew quite well, arrived soon after and, upon hearing the shopkeeper's story, authorized his release.

In some areas of the country, some Asian storeowners had been unceremoniously expelled from the country as unpopular money-grabbing foreigners. Their stores were boarded up and abandoned. The formerly Asian-owned stores were then handed over to local Africans, who soon lost interest in the long hours and lacked the management skills required to make a living from selling *khanga* (a printed cloth worn by African women) or *kaniki* (a black cloth also worn by African women), single cigarettes, and other incidentals to an impoverished population in a remote area. Finally, these windowless stores sat barren under the tropical sun, their previously brightly painted walls fading and their floors littered with droppings of fowl and other birds.

During this uncertain and tumultuous period, the Asians would frequently buy foreign currencies and hoard them, in case they had to flee the country. (The whites, most of whom were expatriates, were allowed to transfer funds legally.) The police and exchange control officials were aware of this widespread practice and at the flimsiest excuse would inspect Asian homes in search of foreign currency. Sometimes they would find it and sometimes they would not be so lucky, as the Asians had mastered quite well the technique of either hiding it or sending it overseas. A few of them had bank accounts in either London or Switzerland, where these funds were deposited in numbered accounts for "rainier days." Living in Africa, one thing they had learned was to always plan ahead and devise methods to overcome regulations.

* * *

Tanganyika, now free of colonialism, turned its attention to another important facet of life: the government soon realized the necessity of reclaiming its arts, songs, dances, culture, and music that had been mutilated by the colonial regime. However free a country might be, it is nothing without its language, traditions, culture, and music. The immediate approach taken by the government of Tanganyika was to recover and recapture the past by creating a special ministry to deal with cultural matters. Nyerere established the new Ministry of National Culture and Youth in his Republic Day speech of December 10, 1962 (the year following independence): "I have done this because I believe that culture is the essence and spirit of any nation. A country that lacks its own culture is no more than a collection of people without the spirit that makes them a nation. Of all the crimes of colonialism there is none worse than the attempt to make us believe we had no indigenous culture of our own; or that what we did have was worthless—something of which we should be ashamed, instead of a source of pride."

The prime minister continued, "When we were at school, we were taught to sing the songs of the European. How many of us were taught the songs of the Wanyamwezi or the Wahehe? Many of us have learned to dance the rumba or the 'chachacha,' to rock-and-roll and to 'twist,' and even to dance the waltz and the foxtrot. But how many of us can dance, have even heard of, the *gombe sugu*, the *mangala*, the *konge nyang'umumi*, *kiduo*, or *lele mama*? Most of us can play the guitar, the piano, or other European musical instruments. How many Africans in

Tanganyika, particularly among the educated, can play the African drums?

"So I have set up this new ministry to help regain our pride in our culture. I want to seek out the best of the traditions and customs of all the tribes and make them part of our national culture."

Young men from rural areas had flocked to the capital after independence in search of work that the fruits of independence were supposed to bring. For young women, the post-independence period opened up a number of opportunities, from domestic employment and secretarial work to relationships with men, including in the sex trade.

Against the background of such an unproductive, undesirable, and vagrant young population which was flourishing in the city, there was a prevalence of youths with "decadent" Western values. The new independent government was forced to conjure up ideas to launch a national culture, which would target and seek to eradicate soul music, beauty contests, and racy films and magazines. The government soon realized that its youths especially were getting out of hand; something had to be done to prevent the decay in young African society.

In October 1968, I witnessed the "Battle of the Minis" in Dar es Salaam, when in the country's sprawling Kariakoo Market a screaming mob halted buses and dragged off

African girls who were wearing tight dresses or miniskirts. The girls were beaten and had their clothes ripped off.

This was the beginning of "cultural revolution," African style. President Nyerere, a disciple of Mao Zedong, had decreed that Tanzania should copy China's Proletariat Revolution, rejecting all things foreign. Nyerere's Green Guards, so called for the colour of their uniforms, targeted miniskirts as their priority item.

Opposition to this campaign came from the University of Dar es Salaam, where co-eds put on their shortest minis and told the Green Guards to "get lost." Girls at a youth hostel unanimously voted that "men should not decide what women should wear." One secretary defended her mini, explaining that it made it easier for her to move around the office and push through a crowded bus. A female member of Parliament supported the miniskirted girls, assuring them that "you can go naked—we won't object."

However, the country's stubborn President Nyerere appeared determined to fight. "It is foolish to wear clothes that show legs," he declared. "It would be better for people to go unclothed if their intention is to expose their legs."

The country's Youth League sided with the president and launched the "Operation *Vijana* [Youth]" campaign to single out miniskirted women. The Youth League extended its ban to include everything symbolizing the "cultural enslavement of the African," such as wigs, tight pants for men or women, and chemicals used to bleach skin and "dehumanize the African people." Hair-straightening devices, lipstick, and other cosmetics had already been condemned. Beauty contests, the "exploitation of female flesh," were declared taboo. To provide an example of how women should dress, the uniforms for female Green Guards—thick skirts worn well below the knees—were considered to be appropriate. Riot police were summoned to the Kariakoo bus station, the capital's main bus depot, to control gangs of youths who were harassing women wearing miniskirts or tight dresses. Tear gas had to be used to disperse them.

During this time I was responsible for editorial pages, including letters to the editor, at the *Standard*. An intense and fierce debate was taking place in the country's newspapers on topics ranging from national culture and gender roles to respectability, indecency, and morality. The local press published 150 letters, sixteen poems, and nineteen editorials on the topic of miniskirts alone.[3]

The Swahili newspaper *Ngurumo* (Thunderstorm) was bombarded with letters from readers expressing their views on miniskirts. One supporter of the anti-mini campaign said the ban had been imposed by the TANU Youth

League (TYL) "to mark their anger at the prostitution being practised by some young ladies who are also members of the UWT [TANU's women's wing]" and that TYL cadres "must be prepared to cut out the minis not only from Kariakoo but even from the hotels where they are harboured." A common target of dress-code attacks were barmaids, who were generally thought to be engaged in the sex trade.

The *Standard*, the country's leading English daily, received 108 letters concerning the ban; only fourteen of these were in favour. Supporters of the ban maintained that miniskirts, tight trousers, and wigs undermined Tanzania's culture and were foreign in nature. Opponents claimed that it was futile to condemn fashion as an imitation of foreign culture—after all, all mass-produced goods were foreign.

"Unless they [the TYL] want to see Tanzanians going naked, they should believe me that we have no fashion in Tanzania which is acceptable as originating from this country. . . . Whatever we choose as our national dress, we shall be deceiving ourselves," one letter writer said.[4]

Many letter writers took jabs at the dress worn at the state banquets by local leaders and political stalwarts, some arguing that "traditional costumes" featured by the national dancing troupes were just as revealing as miniskirts. Others were bold enough to point out that the ruling party's TANU elite, including President Nyerere, had made increasingly popular the "Zhou Enlai suit," which was in itself foreign dress.

However, one correspondent really hit the nail on the head. He pointed out that if the government's intention really was to preserve African culture, then its members should all go half-naked as "our grandfathers used to do." He reminded the officials that all the clothes they wore were "foreign culture," adding that if the government wanted people to preserve *our* culture, then "Why are we telling the Masai tribesmen to stop going half naked and put on modern dress like trousers?"

As a young Tanzanian, I felt that the correspondence in newspapers and the prevalent mood in the country clearly showed that the nation had become modern and mature in its thinking, critical, and fashion conscious. The country was split between the progressives, who didn't mind seeing their women in miniskirts, and the traditionalists, who felt female decency was more important than fashion.

The newly independent government's aim and intention was to create a modern African society, and their measures were aimed at doing so, but political stalwarts such as the Green Guards took the law into their hands and were anxious to implement it.

Further aftermath of independence was the birth of a new tribe in Tanzania. The country was home to approximately 120 tribes, but after independence Tanzania acquired the *wabenzi*—members of the new African ruling class, usually government officials (or their family members). The *wabenzi* were so named because they usually drove imported vehicles, mostly Mercedes Benzes. After *uhuru* there was a proliferation of *wabenzi*, not only in Tanzania, but through most of Africa.

A Mercedes Benz is a status symbol everywhere, but when people became infatuated with the car as a status symbol in impoverished Africa—in countries usually dependent on foreign aid and whose populations faced disease and poverty—buying such luxury vehicles should have been far from their minds. The function and role of a newly independent government was to protect its population and appear to govern without any semblance of extravagance or wastage of public funds.

The *wabenzi* were contradicting what *uhuru* stood for, and the public in general thought that their political leaders were taking the money from foreign governments and pissing it away. In the public's mind, Mercedes Benzes symbolized extravagant spending and an absence of accountability; their presence fostered a lack of public confidence in their leaders.

I am in no way suggesting that everyone who drove a Mercedes Benz in Africa was corrupt, but the public had that perception. I do remember as a high school student, during my two years at the multiracial Aga Khan Boys Secondary School in Dar es Salaam, we would see several Mercedes parked outside, waiting to pick up kids of VIPs—sons, brothers, and relatives of African ministers and top civil servants—while the majority of African students caught a bus to go home. Apparently, the fruits of independence hadn't reached their parents yet. The majority of students would watch enviously as those privileged *wabenzi* kids went home in their air-conditioned vehicles, while they waited in the scorching sun for the bus—the people's car.

National Service or National Servitude?

I'LL NEVER FORGET OCTOBER 22, 1966. THIS WAS THE DAY that changed my whole career and turned my life around. It was the day I was expelled from university for leading a demonstration against compulsory national service for university students.

I was in my final year at the university, majoring in political science. Tanzania's president, Julius Nyerere, was adamant about introducing national service for the country's youths. The government wanted all of them, including university students, to undergo two years of service, which would include three months of military training. During the remaining twenty-one months, recruits were expected to wear the national service uniform—in the classroom if you were a student, or at work, whether in a hospital as a doctor or in court as a lawyer. During those two years, under national service regulations, 60 percent of one's salary was expected to go to the government's national service fund, leaving the wage-earner, including new university graduates, with 40 percent to survive on.

"This is your contribution to your country," the president is reported to have said. But the students were asking a different question: "Is it national service or national servitude?" They were furious. It was a burning issue for them. "How could the government do this? Graduation was supposed to be a happy period in one's life, opening doors to a stable financial future and prosperity," one of my classmates said.

A university degree was considered to be a passport to success for the majority of Tanzanian students, who had dreamt of buying a Volkswagen or a Fiat as soon as they got their first paycheque. Every student aspired to a cushy, well-paid job. Their parents in the villages had aspirations that their sons and daughters, once they completed their university education, would be able to contribute financially to the family. Even members of extended families expected something from their graduating relatives. The government was making a dent in their plans. We felt it had no right to shatter everyone's dreams.

Personally, the issue didn't affect me that much as I came from a middle-class family who would have definitely supported me if I needed financial assistance after graduation. But I considered it my duty as vice-president of the students' union to support the executive and whatever decision was made by the majority of students. The students' union executive tried very hard to negotiate with the minister in charge of national service, Second Vice-President Rashidi Kawawa. They even softened their position and proposed that the government meet the students halfway—splitting the earnings of recruits fifty-fifty. That was a very generous offer, but the government flatly rejected it, sticking to its original sixty-forty plan.

"We can't be dictated to by the government," said the students' union president James Mkoka.

"Listen, Jimmy, that's the government. You can't do anything against them. We have to compromise," I responded.

"Well, we have to take the matter before the general student body and get directions from them as to what they expect the executive to do. After all, we are responsible to them," said the publicity chairman, Saidi Kariboo.

While we were discussing our strategy, a message came from the State House that President Nyerere wanted to see the executive members at his private beach house at Msasani Beach.

The student leadership was elated: the president, Mwalimu himself, wanted to see them and discuss the issue. This was a fantastic opportunity to present their case to the highest authority in the land. This was like speaking to God himself! "Let's go!" was the unanimous decision.

A positive reply was sent to the State House, stating that the students were anxious to meet the president and to discuss the national service issue. We were told to arrive in the afternoon at the residence, located on the Indian Ocean. Our party of six arrived at exactly one o'clock. The president's press secretary, Paul Sozigwa, escorted us to an inner room containing several chairs with large cushions. The walls were adorned with large pictures of Tanzanian wildlife, landscapes, including Mount Kilimanjaro, portraits of Masai warriors, and other scenes. The group sat nervously awaiting the arrival of the president.

Sozigwa chatted with the group, trying to put us at ease. After about ten minutes, a smiling President Nyerere walked in, carrying the foot-long black stick that he usually carried with him at public rallies and functions. The stick was supposed to be his good luck charm, or so was the general belief. He was wearing a Chinese-style collarless black Zhou Enlai suit jacket and matching trousers.

"*Hamu jambo wanainchi,*" he said. "How are you, fellow citizens?"

"We are very well, Mwalimu," replied the students in unison.

Mwalimu, like a teacher being introduced to new pupils, shook hands with everyone and tried to remember our first names. He stopped before me, asking me if I was the university correspondent for the *Standard*.

I said, "Yes, your excellency," and thanked Mwalimu for being so observant—all in Swahili. The president burst out laughing, adding, to my amazement, "This guy is not a *muhindi* (Asian); he is an African!" Everyone joined in the laughter. I was flattered by his remarks.

"*Karibuni!* Welcome!" the president said, taking a centre seat and motioning his guests to sit down. He sat in front of us, with the press secretary by his side. The president looked slimmer in person than in his pictures in newspapers, with grey peppering his curly black hair.

Negotiations began in earnest, and the president of the students' union, James, presented the students' case. Choking with emotion, James said, "Mr. President, we're willing to meet the government halfway, fifty-fifty—" but before he could even finish the sentence, the president had started shaking his head in disapproval. Soon it became very clear that the president was in no mood to change his stance. Like the teacher that he was, he told the delegation, "Look, guys. It is your duty to give back 60 percent of your salary because the nation has educated you and invested in your future. You can live comfortably on 40 percent for two years. This is the sacrifice that your countrymen are asking of you. It is your duty to give back to your country 60 percent of your salary for educating you. Two years will pass in no time, believe me." The majority of students at the university were on government scholarships, which meant that they were contracted to work for the government after graduating. "What's two years in your lifetime?" he asked. "It is not a huge sacrifice that the nation is demanding of you."

The cool breeze that was blowing from the Indian Ocean directly into the presidential palace had no effect on either side. The students still wanted a fifty-fifty deal.

"Mr. President, we students do not deny that it's our duty to contribute to the nation," said another member of our delegation, who had summoned up the courage. "Yes, it's our duty; we recognize that and believe in the principles of national service. In fact, we do feel that we are indebted to the nation for our education, but we believe that 40 percent is very little for us to survive on."

The evening ended cordially, but without any settlement. The president stuck to his guns. "Go and think it over and discuss it with your fellow students. Our position is very clear: sixty-forty and nothing less," the president concluded, sounding as if he had issued a presidential order. We students looked at one another in disbelief. How can you argue with the president of the country? Like young children admonished by their teacher, we uttered some apologetic words and got up to leave. Disappointed and dejected, our delegation left to return to the campus. On our way back, the group sat in utter silence, with the president's ultimatum still ringing in our ears.

The next day, the student population was abuzz with the story of their executive's encounter with the president. The president had told the group to take it or leave it, they were told. How could Mwalimu, who was himself a teacher, treat student representatives like *totos* (children)? "After all, we are the intellectuals of the country and its future leaders," they argued. "How can the president dismiss our demands so frivolously?" A meeting of the general student body was scheduled for the following week to discuss what had transpired during the meeting with the president.

It was well known among students that secret service members were active on the campus. Moreover, some students were related to the president personally, while others belonged to his tribe and were therefore more sympathetic to his line of thinking. They were said to be reporting all discussions and the thinking of the executive to the government. There were also rumours that even the student executive had been infiltrated with "spies." Names of national service "sympathizers" and "opponents" were being fed to the government, or so the rumour went.

These were difficult times for the student leadership. The six of us didn't know who to trust, what to believe, or what to do in this precarious situation. The campus atmosphere was tense. The whole student community was upset and anxious for quick action. The day of the general meeting of the student body arrived. It was held in the evening, after supper, in the main lecture theatre. Students filled the dining hall to have an early supper so as to get good seats at the meeting. Practically everyone was expected. The national service issue affected every student. It was a bread-and-butter issue. Even students from other East African countries came to listen and show their support. They knew that one day they might have to face a similar situation. What Tanzania does today, someone else will be doing tomorrow: this was the thinking. That's the type of reputation the country had. The first East African country to gain independence, Tanzania was the leader—it did things first. Kenya and Uganda usually followed.

Students' union president James Mkoka was expected to make a dynamic speech. The executive had decided to act upon the wishes of the general student body. Students started trickling in an hour in advance. Fifteen minutes before the start of the meeting, James was nowhere to be seen. Word came that he had taken ill and that the vice-president would have to step in.

Though it was hard to believe the story, rumour had it that James had been warned by the secret service that if he went to the meeting, there would be serious repercussions. According to another rumour, the government didn't want the meeting to take place. As vice-president, though unprepared for the occasion, I had to step in at the last moment and save the face of the executive.

Putting on a brave front before a packed house, I walked onto the stage and began: "My fellow students, tonight we have a very important decision to make. It could turn out to be one of the most important decisions of our lives, so please think hard and consider it very carefully before you decide.

"Your executive had a meeting with Mwalimu recently, and we presented your point of view to him. His view is that students should sacrifice for the education that they have received from the government. This is our time to pay back. On your behalf, we presented our fifty-fifty proposal as a last resort, but he wouldn't budge on his terms."

I continued, "The government has put us students in a very precarious position. It has rejected every proposal that we have placed on the table. They want sixty-forty and nothing else. Take it or leave it—that's where we stand today. Sixty percent of the wages will go to the government and 40 percent will come to the student to live on. On this 40 percent, we have to maintain our own family, our parents, and other extended family members. How can we do this? We even asked Mwalimu this. But he wants us to try. He wants us to sacrifice, as he says, for the sake of our nation. Our country demands that sacrifice from us.

"So, my brothers and sisters, we have to decide what course of action to take tonight. The floor is now open for discussion."

Before I had even finished my speech, students wanting to comment had formed a lineup. It was decided for the sake of time that only a few people would be allowed to speak, and then the matter would be put to a vote.

"The government is being very unfair. We should demonstrate and let our feelings be known," said one student, amid thunderous applause.

"It's about time Mwalimu should have some opposition. Let's show it to him," said another angry student.

"If we don't do it now, no one will do it for us. We have had it," said a frustrated speaker. Others just repeated the feeling and echoed the sentiments of previous speakers. No one spoke in favour of the sixty-forty wage split. The issue was then put to a vote, with a unanimous result: there was consensus that students should demonstrate to express their indignation.

The executive was powerless: we had the option of either refusing to carry out the wishes of the student electorate and resigning, or carrying out the students' wishes and organizing the demonstration. We were in a dilemma; we were damned if we did and damned if we didn't. Finally, it was decided the demonstration would be held in two days.

On that day—October 22, 1966—the campus was abuzz with activity early in the morning. Everyone woke up early to catch buses, which were provided as transport to the demonstration, and to meet at a central point in the city designated as the starting point. Buses started taking students from the campus at 7:30 a.m.

The students' union executive, who were transported in my British-made Anglia car (which, in jest, we dubbed the Arusha Declaration, after Nyerere's socialist doctrine, because its license plate was AR 9134), were already at the meeting place, with placards and slogans, trying to organize everything. James stressed to everyone gathered that no one should indulge in violence and that the demonstration should highlight only student demands. He reiterated that if confronted by the police, we should exercise caution at all times. These types of messages were repeatedly conveyed to students.

The demonstration finally started at eleven o'clock, after the last bus had arrived. The majority of those who turned up were Tanzanian students; Kenyans, Ugandans, and other foreigners remained on campus. Some Tanzanian students also stayed at the university, choosing not to participate in the demonstration for whatever reasons, and were branded as traitors.

It was the most impressive united front that the country had seen since independence. In a one-party state where the president was supreme, no one had ever dared to oppose or make any semblance of opposition to the president and his government. Some students carried placards expressing their innermost feelings: "Give students their due," "Don't deny students what they deserve," "Nyerere out of touch with reality," "Gov't killing students' incentives," "Mwalimu has been out of classroom for too long," and so on. Most of the placards displayed personalized attacks on the president, holding him responsible for student frustrations.

Students were very vocal in what they had to say. They were upset and angry that the government had not listened to their demands, and some felt that the politicians themselves were not making enough sacrifices for the nation—that they were preaching sacrifice to students without practising it themselves.

One placard said, "TERMS HARSH—COLONIALISM BETTER." According to later reports, the president, an ardent nationalist, was personally offended when told of this particular placard. I could visualize Nyerere sitting in the State House, saying to himself, "I am the nationalist who fought colonialism and brought independence to this country; here are students who were in their diapers at the time, and only five years after independence they are telling me—the guy who fought for it—that colonialism is better? Come on. They don't know what I, Julius Kambarage Nyerere, have gone through to get independence for this country. Who is this bunch of kids trying to teach? I am *Mwalimu* (teacher) of this country, and do you think my people call me *Baba wa Taifa* (Father of the Nation) for nothing? I will show them. They have no respect for their elders. Elders in African society have a special place: a place of respect and honour. They are giving me no respect by saying colonialism was better!" Not only was Nyerere's pride hurt, it was completely wounded, shattered.

The demonstration had by now arrived at the seashore, on the corner where the Central Establishment and other government offices were located. It was just a block away from the State House. Several civil servants came out of their offices in support and started clapping—though hoping their bosses and ministers would not see them doing so. These workers had never seen a demonstration challenging the government. No one had ever dared oppose the government. Other political parties were banned, and the government had always been supreme. Some thought it was about time someone posed some opposition to the government, and citizens believed the students were very courageous in doing so.

As the students were winding their way through the streets, the city's regional commissioner, Mustapha Songambele, came out and asked them to stop. He informed them that the president wanted all of the demonstrating students to come to the State House. The president wanted to talk to them. The students' union executive met under a tree to digest the president's message and to determine how to respond.

"Do we have a choice?" said one student leader. "Do you know what will happen if we do not go?" asked another. "Go to jail!" someone else offered. After a brief roadside discussion, it was decided to meet the president. With Songambele in the lead and the student leaders beside him, the demonstrators marched towards the State House.

Its huge iron gates opened as the crowd came closer. Inside, the inspector general of police, Ali Hashimu, met

Songambele. The beautiful lawns of the State House looked as if they had recently been mowed and trimmed. Policemen armed with guns surrounded the students as they innocently entered the grounds. The police chief's voice came over the loudspeaker, asking students to sit down on the grass. In front, several chairs and a desk had already been placed, presumably for Mwalimu and some of his accompanying ministers. Students sat on the lawn, surrounded by the armed policemen. No one had a good feeling about what was to come, and everyone was nervous.

In a few minutes, one of the doors of the State House opened and a stone-faced Mwalimu, wearing his usual Zhou Enlai suit and followed by an entourage of seven ministers, marched towards the chairs. The whole group appeared angry. The air was so tense that one could even hear the leaves in nearby trees crackling.

Mwalimu took the centre chair, and his entourage—which included Vice-President Kawawa, who had the national service portfolio, and several other senior ministers—took their places. The president looked straight ahead and, without any of the introductory remarks or pleasantries that usually reflected his jovial personality, blurted out what he had to say: "So you students want your pound of flesh, eh?"

He continued, "Today you have come here to demand your dues, forgetting that this country has paid for your education. You are being ungrateful to your country, to the nation, and its citizens. All these years, we have educated you, spent money, lots of money, so that this country can benefit. We wanted to move forward, be more independent of foreigners. Foreign manpower. They are still here in our schools, hospitals, factories, and civil service. You still want Tanzania to be dependent on foreigners? You students are being ungrateful.

"And you want your pound of flesh?" he shouted, repeating the sentence and looking visibly annoyed. "This country does not deserve this kind of treatment from its educated class, from its intelligentsia. We wanted you to sacrifice two years of your lives, and you refuse it. After all that your country has done for you. Paid for your education. Now you want your pound of flesh? Eh? You don't know what independence means. This country is still relying on foreign manpower. It's still not self-sufficient in manpower, and you students don't understand that."

The president continued, "I shall take nobody—not a single person—into this national service whose spirit is not in it . . . so make your choice. I'm not going to spend public money to educate anybody who says national service is a prison. . . . Is this what the citizens of this country worked for? . . . You are demanding a pound of flesh. Everybody is demanding a pound of flesh except the poor peasant. What kind of country are we building? The nation says to its youth, 'We want your service,' and the youth does not then turn to the nation and say, 'For how much?'"

As the president spoke, his ministers nodded their approval. After taking almost an hour to hammer the same subject, the president came to an abrupt halt. "Inspector," he said, addressing the chief of police. "Send these students home!"

"Very well, sir!" Hashimu responded.

Mwalimu got up and, followed by his entourage, walked into the State House without uttering another word. All the students, not knowing what to make of the president's utterances, stood up en masse, thinking that was the end of the dreadful meeting and that they could now disperse and return to the campus.

Inspector Hashimu, who obviously had received orders ahead of time, went to the microphone and ordered everyone to sit down. He knew exactly what the president had meant. "You students, sit down wherever you are. You are asked to sit down. Please sit down! Sit down."

His voice was angry and authoritative—as if he were now imposing martial law. Everyone sat down as they were ordered. He instructed all students to line up to be photographed individually and fingerprinted by police personnel, who were already there for that purpose. Police with guns were stationed all around the State House, and there was nothing we unarmed students could do. We couldn't believe it.

The police chief's voice came on the loudspeaker again: "Now for the second step. I want all of you students to group yourselves according to the towns and villages you come from. Go to your hometowns. I want all the students from Morogoro, Moshi, Arusha, Tanga, Mwanza, Tabora, and so on to line up near those buses with the community names written on them. You will go to the university in these buses, pick up your luggage and other personal belongings, and go home to your parents—today!"

Students were dumbfounded. "Is this really happening?" we wondered. "How could they do this?" Was Mwalimu—the teacher, the educator, and the nationalist who brought independence, the Father of the Nation—throwing students out of university and sending them home? This was unbelievable. "Are we being expelled from university?" This question was on everyone's mind. "And if so, for how long?" Nothing seemed clear.

This couldn't be happening in our country, we thought. By doing this, was the president not delaying the progress of the country? Would we not be going backwards?

These type of things happened in Communist regimes, not in democracies, even if it was a so-called one-party democracy. I, along with the students around me, was confused. Some were crying. The situation was bewildering. When I looked around, I saw James sitting two rows ahead of me. Our eyes met. We looked at each other and shook our heads in disbelief. What could we do?

Students whispered and murmured to one another about the president's uncharacteristic behaviour, but then all of a sudden the commotion died down, followed by an eerie silence. Some were crying uncontrollably, others were sweating, and some were just dumbfounded. There was confusion all around. The students were shocked, in disbelief. I had worshipped Mwalimu Nyerere. He was my philosopher king. His books—published by Oxford University Press and containing all his speeches, from pre-independence days till then—adorned my bookcase. My hero Mwalimu was not capable of doing this sort of thing, but he had done it. He had suddenly fallen in my estimation because of this unforgivable action. People change, I told myself. I remembered from my political science class Lord Acton, who said, "Power corrupts, absolute power corrupts absolutely." I thought I was witnessing a classic example.

The police chief and his deputies kept on repeating their message, blaring it over the loudspeaker. We soon found out there would be special treatment for the students' union executive. We were identified, singled out, and taken separately in a special police van to the city's central police station, where we were questioned individually about our part in the demonstration. Or, more correctly, we were interrogated: Whose idea was it to organize the demonstration? Were the students instigated by a foreign power? Did we receive any help from leaders of the student power movement in the United States?

This was the time of student power. In the 1960s, the United States faced one of its most turbulent times when university students became politically active. This was the era of the civil rights and antiwar movements, and many believed that student participation in these movements changed the face of American society.

In Dar es Salaam, the police were desperate to know who exactly had suggested that students should demonstrate against the government. We didn't know that we were going to be asked this question, but the executive stood united and we each answered that we were bound by a students' union motion to demonstrate—and that was the truth. It was the will of the whole student body, we maintained unanimously.

The six members of the students' union executive had to spend the night in police custody; that meant giving up our comfortable beds on campus to be guests of the government at the central police station, sleeping in cells usually reserved for prisoners being held overnight pending their hearings. Each of us was locked in a separate cell, each with a bare wooden bed and small open toilet.

I sat in my tiny cell, remembering and analyzing the day's events. I was thinking about what my colleagues must be doing and thinking. I couldn't sleep that night, as so much had happened. I kept thinking about what Mahatma Gandhi must have endured in his cell the many times he was imprisoned, first in South Africa, and then later during the British Raj in India, though I am in no way comparing myself to the great Mahatma. Although I was not fighting for independence, it almost felt like I was! In South Africa and India, it was British colonialists, a foreign power, subjugating the people, but here our own nationalist government was doing it. It just didn't make sense.

The next day we were released, and upcountry students were given bus vouchers to go home as the buses carrying the other students had left the previous day. Two armed policemen took me home, because my parents lived in Dar es Salaam. When my father opened the door, one of the policemen asked him, point-blank, "Is this your son?"

Frightened, Dad could barely utter yes. The policeman said, "He has been a very naughty boy. You'd better take good care of him," and he pushed me towards the door. My father was relieved to see me unharmed and safe at home, but I received an exhaustive and lengthy lecture on why I should not get involved in student politics.

The next day's newspapers carried front-page stories about the students' demonstration and its aftermath. "Mwalimu sends students home," said one newspaper headline. "Mwalimu shuts down university," said another. "Tanzanian U students expelled," declared a third one.

Local and foreign commentators had a field day. They initiated a postmortem of the student demonstration. Why did it happen? Who was responsible for it? Some commentators maintained that the students had adopted "attitudes of superiority," had betrayed the nation, and deserved to be punished. Others suggested that perhaps it was the influence and teaching of a number of radical expatriate scholars whom the university had attracted, especially in the Faculty of Arts and Social Sciences, who were responsible for spreading radical thoughts on the campus. At the time, the faculty included professors who were branded radical. Needless to say, none of these professors were involved in influencing students.

In the years following the demonstration, as Dar es Salaam law and development studies professor Haroub Othman described it, the campus became "the epicentre of radicalism on the African continent. In the ten-year period from 1967 to 1977, the university was a major cooking pot of ideas, and provided a splendid platform for debate and discussion. No African scholar, leader or freedom fighter could ignore its environs."[5] During this time, as Professor Issa Shivji has noted, the University of Dar es Salaam developed into one of the most well-known universities in Africa, if not the world. A number of foreign students, including white and African-American students from the United States, pursued their education at the institution.

But at the end of 1966, the implications of the president's order gradually started to sink in. The country's highest institution of learning was without its own students—the Tanzanians who had demonstrated. Students of other nationalities were there, as well as the small percentage of Tanzanians who had chosen not to participate in the march. These students had the pleasure of the whole university to themselves as classes ran at about one-tenth of their capacity. The atmosphere at the university was one of fear and suspicion. Students didn't trust anyone, especially the remaining Tanzanians, who were suspected of being government "spies" or "agents" or "collaborators." It was an appalling atmosphere in an institution of higher learning aimed at promoting free speech and producing liberal thinkers and the nation's future leaders.

Two weeks after the demonstration, the government issued a statement banning the Tanzanian Students' Union, branding the executive "ringleaders," and blaming them for organizing the protest. The government wanted scapegoats. Since only James and I remained in Dar, it fell upon the two of us to dispose of the files and other property of the banned union. After a few days, James left for Nairobi to apply for a job with the East African Community, since he rightly feared he would not get a job in Tanzania. We shook hands and wished each other well.

It was a time to reflect. Did the national service really affect me personally? I felt that the 40 percent of any wages that the government was going to let me keep after graduation wouldn't really have mattered greatly to me, since I would have family resources to fall back on. But it was in my nature always to fight for the underdog. As a student leader, I had considered it my duty to go along with the majority of the students, who had resolved to demonstrate. That support and camaraderie cost me my higher education and degree. I was in my final year of a Bachelor of Arts degree in political science. When the expulsion from the university came, I had only a political science dissertation and couple of other things to finalize before sitting for my finals, just a few months away.

I had had in mind a career in foreign service, followed later on by politics. I had already applied for a foreign affairs posting and had received word that I was to be provisionally assigned to Addis Ababa, Ethiopia, as a third secretary in the Tanzanian embassy. As Tanzanian students, the majority of us were on government scholarships, which stipulated that we would join the government after graduating. As a very nationalistic-minded person, I'd had ambitions to go into politics in the future, possibly to replace the second generation of Asian ministers in the Tanzanian cabinet.

But that was not to be my destiny. I had been branded "ringleader" for my part in the student demonstration, and the country's biggest employer, the government, was not about to give me a job. Since I had been a university correspondent for the *Standard*, I decided to try my luck at the paper. I went to see its British editor, Brandon Grimshaw, who was very sympathetic. He had seen my work and, without any modesty, he was impressed with my writing skills. The following week, I started as a reporter at the *Standard*. Journalism had replaced foreign service and politics.

With a strong command of English, a university education, and a sound understanding of the local political system, I did very well in journalism, writing stories, features, and in-depth articles. The managing editor, Kenneth Ridley, who was usually confined to his office, came out several times to personally congratulate me for my well-written stories. I was flattered. Soon I became a star reporter. I was assigned to cover VIPs arriving at the airports and events conducted in English. Political rallies, the parliament, city council debates, and other public meetings were conducted in Swahili, which had become Tanzania's official language.

During my assignments, I had the pleasure of meeting President Nyerere several times. Whenever he saw me, he would always make it a point to greet me, always with a smile: "*Habari gani, Bwana Ladha?*" (What's new, Mr. Ladha?).

I would reply, "*Mzuri sana, Mwalimu!*" (Very well, Mwalimu!)

The fact that he had expelled me from university as one of those so-called ringleaders didn't seem to matter when we met in later years. Perhaps he had either forgotten or forgiven me. That was my theory. It never became an issue.

Life as a Journalist

ONE MORNING, BRANDON GRIMSHAW, THE *STANDARD*'S editor, sent me to the Tanzania Information Services office to fetch a press release the government was issuing on expelled students. President Nyerere had decided to pardon the students who, one year earlier, had demonstrated against the national service. I was obviously an interested party.

As soon as I got the package, which contained a list of pardoned students, I started flipping pages, searching for my name, but I couldn't find it. I returned to the intro of the press release, and there I read that President Nyerere had pardoned all expelled students except the six "ringleaders," which, of course, included me. For a moment, I froze. The government was unnecessarily making a scapegoat of us. I felt pity for myself and disgust at this treatment.

How could the president be so ruthless? Did he have no compassion? He had already cost us a year. Wasn't that punishment enough? Indeed, the wrath of the president had no limits, no bounds! He was merciless and insensitive.

Disappointed, dejected, and deep in my thoughts, I returned to the newspaper office and told Grimshaw of the news contained in the press release. "Now I can't go back to the university," I said with a sad face, tears welling up.

The editor looked at me in a fatherly manner, placed his hand on my shoulder, and said, "You have nothing to worry about, bud. We are your family and you have made good progress with us. We'll take care of you. This is your home. Welcome to the *Standard* family." He smiled. "Mansoor, drink a glass of water, compose yourself, and write the story. It's your story, bud," he said and then vanished into his office.

Yes, I became the story. In that emotionally drained condition, I sat in front of my typewriter, took a deep breath, and started typing the first sentences of the story for the next morning's edition:

> President Julius Nyerere yesterday pardoned over 230 Tanzanian university students who were expelled last October for demonstrating against the government's policy of national

> service. Excluded in the presidential pardon were the six members of the Tanzania university student union executive, who were branded by the government as ringleaders, and blamed for organizing the demonstration.

While writing the story, I had to keep my personal feelings and emotions in check. The piece made the next morning's front page with my byline. It was perhaps one of the most difficult stories of my career thus far. Considering the story affected me personally, it was difficult to write. I was glad it didn't make me cry. After I finished the piece, the editor took me to the city's popular Gymkhana Club—where non-whites had once been barred—for a drink. He instilled in me that journalism is a great career and that I had a great future in it. He also said once you worked with the *Standard*, you could work anywhere in the world. (Looking back now, I see how true those prophetic words have been.) His soothing words were a great comfort to me then.

It was during this time when I was a reporter with the *Standard* that Nyerere had a feud with one of his lieutenants, Home Minister Oscar Kambona, who fled to Britain in self-imposed exile in 1967. For months the government was silent, making no public statement on the issue.

One afternoon, Vice-President Rashidi Kawawa was scheduled to present certificates to national service graduating students at the Mgulani Camp, and the reporter expected to cover it was delayed somewhere. I happened to be in the office and so was assigned to cover the story, normally a simple, straightforward, picture-taking ceremony. I was told that I would only need to gather cutline information. Traditionally, no speeches were made at such functions.

I went there with photographer Adarsh Nayar, and to everyone's amazement, the vice-president took the opportunity to make a speech in Swahili and talk about Kambona's disappearance from Tanzania. Being a Zanzibar-born Asian, my Swahili was considered better than that of most Asians, though I had not taken any Swahili courses in school. In his speech, Kawawa said Kambona had fled the country with "bags full of money" and compared him to "a prostitute." It was tough to translate the VP's speech to English while he was speaking in Swahili, and it turned out to be a difficult assignment.

When I got back to the office, Grimshaw apologized for having sent me; he obviously hadn't known Kawawa would speak about the controversial issue—one the country very much wanted to hear about. The paper had to rely on my Swahili to run the story, which appeared on the front page with a nice big byline. I told the editor he would have to take a chance on my translation skills and that both of us could end up in jail the next day. Fortunately, my Swahili won the day!

Within less than a year, I was promoted to sub-editor (called a copy editor in North America), joining several expatriate Brits and two Africans on the desk. This gave me a well-rounded experience. We had a small copy desk and, as copy editors, we had to edit stories, write headlines, do page layout, and once every month we were put in charge as duty editors and expected to send the paper "to bed."

One incident when I was duty editor still stands out. Late one evening in 1968, I received a call from the former speaker of the Tanganyika Legislative Assembly, Abdulkarim Yusufali Alibhai Karimjee, who was a prominent member of the Bohra community, a sect within the Ismaili branch of Shia Islam. That afternoon, the Tanzanian government had expelled the Bohra community's spiritual leader, His Holiness Syedna Dr. Mohammed Burhanuddin, on charges of contravening exchange control regulations of the country.

The new Bohra constitution accorded the Syedna absolute control over the income and assets of Bohras all around the world through a network of *aamils* (priests) who were not answerable to local members of the community. It was believed that under this arrangement Bohras paid significant tithes, which reportedly went into the private coffers of the Syedna. Part of the money found its way into his foreign accounts, while part was spent on his family's extravagant lifestyle.

Karimjee, who obviously knew the *Standard*'s editor, Grimshaw, demanded to talk to him, but I told the former speaker that I was the duty editor and that I would be more than happy to assist him. After a brief discussion, he relented and asked me if there was any possibility that the story of Syedna's expulsion from Tanzania could be taken out of the paper. I was surprised at such a request. I politely told him that it would be going on page one, with pictures, and there was no way that such an important story could be killed.

He still insisted on speaking to Grimshaw, who, he thought, would cooperate with him, but I told Karimjee that my editor was not in the office and that, as the editor on duty, I was the only newspaper official he could talk to. Needless to say, the story of the Syedna's expulsion ran, creating a huge outcry in the country.

After a brief stint on the copy desk, I won a Commonwealth scholarship to study advanced journalism at Cardiff, Wales, offered by Lord Thomson of Fleet Street. As

Britain was considered to be a mecca for journalists, I was quite proud of the honour. I was the envy of some of my former classmates who had returned to Dar University to get their degrees and ended up as civil servants, shuffling documents. In contrast, here I was—a person with no degree who was progressing in a meaningful career.

When I arrived in Cardiff for my studies, my new colleagues were surprised to see me: they had been expecting a black man from Africa. "But you are not black," one of them told me bluntly. I had to explain how this Indian-looking man happened to come from Africa. As it turned out, the journalism course in Cardiff gave me a career boost and a great insight into the profession.

Meanwhile, the *Standard* was becoming more politicized. Political indoctrination classes and marches were introduced. One of the paper's copy boys, Shabani, became the TANU cell leader in the editorial department. His duty was to ensure that all employees attended the marches, and he would chant "Chaka, chaka chinja" to boost everyone's spirits (the phrase is difficult to translate, but essentially means "Cheer up, hurrah, hurrah"). I attended the first few marches, but soon considered them a waste of time and energy. Every African member of the staff was asked to line up in the street in preparation for the march, which was followed by political training.

Shabani, who was usually broke, used to regularly borrow money from me, so I reminded him that if he intended to continue using my services as his customary moneylender, then I would have to be excused from these marches. He readily agreed. At the duly appointed time, I would vanish to the bathroom while the local staff emptied the office for the great march, in the name of socialism and nation building.

There was serious resentment among the editorial staff of this kind of treatment, but in a one-party state they had no choice if they wanted to keep their jobs.

I joined the *Standard* in 1966 and enjoyed four years there before the paper was nationalized in 1970. Then a new code of behaviour was put in place for local journalists, as the government was strengthening its hold in the country, especially on the press. Every local journalist was expected to become a member of TANU, the ruling political party, and participate in the marches.

Nyerere nationalized the *Standard* on February 5, 1970, taking over control from the multinational London-Rhodesian Company (Lonrho) and removing editor Brandon Grimshaw, replacing him with Fred Ngungo, a South African refugee. Ngungo was among a group of South Africans who had taken refuge in Tanzania following President Nyerere's invitation to all nationalist movements to set up their headquarters in Dar es Salaam. Ngungo, who had no newspaper experience, had been publisher of a political magazine, in which then African nationalist leaders such as Kenneth Kaunda, Tom Mboya, Hastings Banda, Joshua Nkomo, Ben Kiwanuka, and others had contributed articles. The magazine was popular among nationalists and freedom fighters since it provided a platform for Pan-African and anticolonial views. This unqualified editor's appointment pleased nobody, but the staff decided to give him a chance and see what would happen. Grimshaw was transferred to the National Development Corporation (NDC), a parastatal organization whose chairman was George Kahama. Once Ngungo occupied the editor's chair he started making decisions, but Mwalimu Nyerere acted as our non-executive editor-in-chief.

After nationalization, both English-language newspapers belonged to the government—the *Standard* and the *Nationalist*. These, and their Kiswahili sister *Uhuru*, then existed as organs of the ruling party, TANU.

The *Standard* had started as a colonial newspaper and was read mostly by the British expatriate community, the Asian business class, and educated Asians and Africans. It had gradually established itself as a leading voice in the country. TANU started its own paper, the *Nationalist*, in 1964, but it was in no way near the *Standard* in terms of quality and editorial excellence. The *Nationalist* mainly carried party propaganda and usually aroused the masses by publishing anti-Asian editorials.

With nationalization, a new era in Tanzania's journalism began. The "President's Charter" was printed on the front page of the *Standard* on February 5, 1970, and it stood as the country's journalism creed until the 1990s:

> Today Tanzania's new "Standard" is born. Government has taken the newspaper into public hands and appointed its own editor. In the future there can be no suspicion that this English-language newspaper is serving the interests of foreign private owners. . . . In accordance with the Arusha Declaration, it is clearly impossible for the largest daily newspaper in independent Tanzania to be left indefinitely in the hands of a foreign company. In a country committed to building socialism, it is also impossible for such an influential medium to be left indefinitely in the control of non-socialist, capitalist owners. The reasons for the Government's decision to acquire the "Standard" are thus both nationalistic and socialistic;

we want Tanzanians to have control of this newspaper. . . .

The new "Standard" will give general support to the policies of the Tanzanian Government, but will be free to join in the debate for and against any particular proposals put forward for the consideration of the people, whether by the Government, by Tanu, or by other bodies. Further, it will be free to initiate discussions on any subject relevant to the development of a socialist society in Tanzania. It will be guided by the principle that free debate is an essential element of true socialism, and it will strive to encourage and maintain a high standard of socialist discussion. The new "Standard" will be free to criticize any particular acts of individual Tanu or Government leaders, and to publicise any failures in the community, by whomever they are committed. . . . The "Standard" editor will be appointed by the President and will have full autonomy in the day-to-day operation of the newspaper. Until such time as the editorial Board is appointed, the new "Standard" will receive directives on editorial policy, on employment policies, and on other matters,

> only from the President of the United Republic, to whom the editor will be exclusively and directly responsible. The watchword of the new socialist "Standard" of Tanzania will be: "The Socialist Equality and Dignity of Man." It is in that spirit that it will seek to serve the citizens of this United Republic, without distinction on grounds of race, religion, sex or tribe.

One of the first decisions Ngungo made was to bring in his socialist-minded friends. Among these prized individuals were Richard Gott, a well-known socialist writer from Britain's *Guardian* newspaper and a specialist in Latin American affairs, and Tony Hall, a South African journalist who had worked at the *Nation* in Kenya. Other left-leaning recruits were Iain Christie and Rod Prince. The rumour in town was that the paper was now full of communists.

Soon after Ngungo took over, his philosophy started to clash with that of the personnel in editorial meetings. Ngungo was inexperienced in daily newspaper journalism and his shallow knowledge of newspaper technicalities showed very clearly. An experienced expatriate British editor described him as the worst editor he had ever encountered, both in his lack of knowledge and his inability to handle people. Under Ngungo, the newspaper changed its mission from delivering news to spreading socialist propaganda. In fact, non-African sub-editors used to play games with Ngungo in which they would use newspaper terminology around him but get the terms slightly wrong—simply for the fun of hearing Ngungo use those terms incorrectly but quite confidently later on.

After the takeover, the sub-editors were especially in turmoil. Previously, the *Standard* had been used to getting its international stories from Reuters only. The new regime had added Prensa Latina (the Cuban news agency), the Africa Research Group, the Associated Press, Xinhua (the Chinese news agency) and TASS (the Russian news agency). This placed a considerable strain on the sub-editors who had to edit the same story using sources with different ideologies.

There was also a directive that we were to change the writing style of our articles to appease socialist political ideologies. For example, "Viet Cong" was to be changed to "Liberation Forces" and the word "terrorist" was to become "freedom fighter."

Nyerere's choice of editor became very unpopular with the *Standard* staff, both local and expatriate, who quickly discovered the limitations of Ngungo's newspaper expertise. The newspaper was technically under the NDC, the economic arm of the government, but the *Standard* also had a direct link with the State House: the president's press secretary, Paul Sozigwa, was often seen coming in and out of the newspaper office. There was no doubt that the president himself was kept abreast of the unrest among the staff and that every move within the office was somehow transmitted to the authorities.

Three members of the staff, including myself, had worked at the *Standard* before nationalization; we had been working as understudies and were due for promotions. Everyone in the office knew this. Two Africans were trainee copy editors, and I was understudying a British expatriate who was the features editor. With the changing of the guards, however, it fell on Ngungo to make decisions about advancements.

Ngungo announced the promotions of the two Africans but not mine. Then he abruptly brought in an African reporter to be trained to work on features with me. I had worked hard for the advancement and felt I deserved it and should have got it. Being passed over was unfair and unbelievably insulting. It was not in my nature to accept rebuffs of any kind from anyone, especially one that targeted me personally. I had stood for fairness with an unblemished record of selflessness while at university. I participated in a protest march against Rhodesia when

Ian Smith's white government made its Unilateral Declaration of Independence, and I had fought against South Africa's apartheid policies. Was I to keep quiet when I believed that I was being discriminated against? I decided to confront Ngungo. At the first opportunity, I rushed into his office and asked him why I had not been promoted.

He responded patronizingly, saying I had to realize that Tanzania was an African country and that Africans, therefore, had to be in the forefront. After all the years of colonial rule, they were now running the show, and everyone was expected to make sacrifices to help them rebuild the country. This was the gist of his explanation.

I couldn't believe what I was hearing. This man, a so-called champion of freedom fighters who supposedly fought apartheid and racism in South Africa, was preaching racism to me. I was baffled, confused, and in utter disbelief. He had failed to be impartial by not giving the job to the most experienced person and was blatantly denying me the promotion because of the colour of my skin.

My inner voice said, rather admonishingly, *Mansoor, don't be a fool. You are a brown person in a black society, and no matter how hard you try to mingle with the majority of blacks, you will always be treated differently because of your colour. And you have the wrong colour. You do not belong here, whether you were born here or not. Don't you get it? You have been wasting your time trying to be accepted, but you haven't been accepted, and you will never be accepted. Get it through your thick head. Haven't you learned enough lessons?*

As I took a few moments to formulate a response, my thoughts continued to assail me: *You fought for the majority of African students while at the university. Sixty percent or 50 percent—why did you care? Now you don't even have a degree. And all those students went back and got theirs. You are fighting a losing battle, you idiot!*

Then suddenly I heard myself speaking: "Mr. Ngungo, do you realize that I am a third-generation Asian born in Tanzania and a citizen of this country? This makes me equal to the Africans who are born here. I have rights equal to the trainee you have chosen for the features department."

I told him that I was amazed to note that he—a so-called nationalist, freedom fighter, anti-racist activist and human rights advocate—was, today, preaching racism to me. He was not practising what he had been preaching all his life! I reminded him that he had left his country fighting discrimination, apartheid, and racism, and I told him frankly that I felt he was discriminating against me because I happened to be of a different colour than native Tanzanians. That he, of all people, was practising double standards. I pointed out this hypocrisy.

Angrily, I told him I was giving him one month to reconsider. I gave him a virtual ultimatum: if I didn't hear from him by then, I said, I'd be out of there. And without waiting for a response, I barged out of his office.

Everyone in the newsroom knew I had gone to see Ngungo. They were curious to find out what had transpired between us. I told them of our discussion and of my ultimatum. They were flabbergasted. There was general agreement among my colleagues that the position I had taken was right—promotion or no promotion, I had made up my mind to show Ngungo he ought not to underestimate me.

However, I had a feeling his decision would not be in my favour. I decided not to wait a month for his answer. The blatant discrimination was the last straw, but I also couldn't reconcile the fact that journalists had to buy party memberships to keep their jobs secure. I believed that one should have a newspaper job because one was a good journalist, and not because one had membership in the ruling party or had the right colour of skin. With deep regret and a heavy heart, I made up my mind to leave my beloved Tanzania.

The following week, I phoned the managing editor of the *Daily Nation* in Nairobi, Kenya, inquiring if the paper had any openings for sub-editors. I was invited for an interview. On my day off, I flew to Nairobi, had an excellent interview, and was offered the job on expatriate terms—that is, with furnished housing and better pay—but was told to wait for a work permit for which the newspaper had to apply. I returned to Dar es Salaam having accomplished my mission. I didn't tell anyone that I was leaving, but immersed myself in work.

Meanwhile, Ngungo continued to make blunders, becoming increasingly unpopular. Discontent in the office grew, and it was only a matter of time before something would happen that would require his being dealt with. That opportunity came when an editorial on Sudanese president Gaafar Mohamed el-Nimeiri was published. In 1970, el-Nimeiri, who had assumed power in a coup the previous year, was facing strong opposition to his new government. He responded with violence, including airstrikes against an opposition base in southeastern Sudan at Aba Island, during which an estimated three thousand people were killed.

In an editorial commentary, the newspaper accused el-Nimeiri of horrendous murder. When the paper hit the stands, TANU's right wing—led by Kawawa, now the prime minister—was up in arms. They demanded Ngungo be sacked immediately because el-Nimeiri, they claimed, was a good friend of Tanzania. Nyerere had to act.

President Nyerere immediately telephoned George Kahama and gave him instructions to deal with Ngungo. Ngungo's day of reckoning had arrived. At about eleven o'clock, Kahama came to the office, and everyone in the newsroom knew something was afoot. Kahama went into Ngungo's office, closed the door, and told him that the president was very upset about the editorial in that morning's paper.

Kahama said the president had instructed him to ask Ngungo to empty his desk drawers and clear the office of all his personal belongings and to escort him home. From there, Ngungo was to pack his bags and leave immediately for the airport, where he was to catch a flight to London—because he was being deported from the country. These were direct orders from the president, Kahama disclosed.

Ngungo was shocked and speechless. He had held one of the most important positions in the country, but in the flicker of a second he was nobody. It took him a while to digest this. He realized there was no escape. The presidential message was direct, firm, and authoritative. Ngungo picked up a glass of water from his desk and asked Kahama if he could have a moment alone. Kahama walked out of the office and into the office of the assistant managing editor, Sammy Mdee. He told Sammy of the president's orders, also informing him that he was now in charge as acting managing editor.

A few minutes later, Ngungo left the office, briefcase in hand, accompanied by Kahama, without uttering a word to anyone. With their backs turned, the staff chuckled with delight and sighed with relief at the end of an unhappy chapter in their working lives. Many felt like clapping but resisted the temptation, happy in the thought that this man's reign of disaster had finally come to an end. Ngungo was taken to his executive bungalow at Oyster Bay, in the upper-class section of Dar es Salaam, where he packed his bags; later, as persona non grata, he boarded an evening flight to England.

As soon as Sammy emerged from his office and came to the newsroom, beaming with pride, everyone clapped and congratulated him on his appointment. "Thanks, my friends," he said. "Don't forget, I'll need the full support of all of you in this position. These are tremendous responsibilities, and I cannot discharge them without your support. So let's work harder and support each other." He added, "Thanks again and let's get back to work. *Uhuru ni kazi* (Independence means work)."

The next day was a different day—the dawn of a new era. The office had an air of optimism and enthusiasm. A week went by and then Sammy called me into his office.

He said he was aware of the injustice that had been done to me, that I had been passed over for a promotion.

He went on: "Well, one of my first duties as acting managing editor was to recommend to the State House that you be appointed features editor, with immediate effect. I have this letter, signed by the president, confirming your appointment. Congratulations!"

"Sorry," I said, "but wrong timing, my friend Sammy, Mr. Managing Editor. I am sorry—I cannot accept it."

"Why not? Why not?"

"Sammy, my dear, dear friend, how can I explain? I am joining the *Daily Nation* in Nairobi. I am expected to start soon," I explained. "Had I known there would be changes here, I would not have applied for another job. But now it's too late. I am committed."

"Don't go, my friend. Don't leave us," Sammy responded. "We need you here. Your country needs you," he added, knowing full well the nationalist angle might sway me as I was known for my nationalistic fervour and loyalty to the country. It was because of my loyalty that when Ngungo had treated me as a second-class citizen, in favour of a black person, I had felt insulted. How dare he have doubted my citizenship and my loyalty to the country?

I interrupted Sammy and said, "Please don't bring the nationhood angle into this argument. I have sacrificed my life and my career for my country, but I have been screwed in the process. I was never appreciated for my loyalty. Ngungo ignored my loyalty and downgraded my citizenship. In his view, an African's citizenship and birthright are better, superior to mine.

"My university education was interrupted because I sympathized with the majority of African students. I didn't give a damn if I got 60 percent or 40 percent of my salary after graduation. It was immaterial to me. Where did my camaraderie and my leadership of the university students' union take me? No degree and an unfinished education. That's the price I had to pay for being too nationalistic, too sympathetic to the majority cause," I said, with tears. "And where were you all when I was blatantly discriminated against here in the office? Did any of you raise your voices? Where were your editorials on racism then?"

Sammy hugged me and told me to calm down. "Promise me you will consider it seriously and think it over. Here, have a drink of water," he said offering me a glass.

All I could do was nod. I left his office wiping my eyes. But there was nothing to think about. I had made a commitment to another employer, a newspaper that had already applied for a work permit for me. The matter had gone too far. The following week, I received a call from the

Daily Nation informing me my work permit had arrived and they were sending some papers, including a two-year contract, for me to sign and return. I was expected to start, as arranged, on January 2, 1971.

Political and personal survival made it necessary for my wife and me to leave at that time. Of course, leaving family and friends, relationships built over a number of years, and uprooting myself from familiar surroundings were major drawbacks, but we had made up our minds and now had to move quickly, and with courage.

The final week at the *Standard* was the most difficult time for me. Farewell parties and goodbyes to old friends and colleagues were not easy. These were sad days, but amid fond memories. There were emotional moments, teary eyes, speechlessness, handshakes, and hugs. I left Tanzania, the country that I loved and cherished, with mixed emotions, but ready to face the new life that lay ahead in Kenya. On the flight to Nairobi I became emotional as I watched the Tanzanian landscape vanish and the Kenyan landscape emerge. I didn't know whether I was leaving Tanzania temporarily or permanently. I couldn't help thinking of the song "Don't Cry for Me, Argentina"—and I hummed, "Don't cry for me, Tanzania!"

I have always believed that one should never look back and regret the past, that one should always look forward to what is ahead, that the future is usually brighter than the past.

Once in Nairobi, Anaar, Hanif, and I stayed in a hotel for a week, courtesy of my new employer, before moving into our three-bedroom home on the outskirts of the city, in Westlands, with quarters for servants. My wife couldn't work in Nairobi because as a foreigner one needed a work permit, applied for by an employer. However, with a young child to look after, the arrangement suited us fine.

Our two-year-old son's nanny, Elizabeth, was an attractive young woman who, unknown to us at first, dated the driver of the minister of economic affairs. One day, by chance, I saw the ministerial car, identifiable by its licence plates, dropping off Elizabeth late at night. The next day we began treating Elizabeth like royalty. With that kind of connection, she could have got us deported on any pretext—or had me appointed as ambassador to Turkey!

Our house had a beautiful garden and a lawn in front, with lots of trees and flowers. A gardener looked after the property. It was a comfortable life in comparison to the life we'd had in Tanzania. With a bell by our bedside, we could summon our servants anytime we needed them. I, a former acclaimed socialist, was learning to live like an expatriate *mzungu* (white man) in a capitalist country.

It was then that I suddenly realized why the whites were so reluctant to leave newly independent African countries to return to England, or wherever it was they'd come from. They were *bwana kubas* (big bosses) in Africa, leading comfortable lives.

The bustling city of Nairobi was very modern and sophisticated compared to laid-back Dar es Salaam. And to get a true sense of it, even today, one has to experience a ride in a *matatu* or "the people's car," as I used to call it. Doing so allows you to experience the real feeling of Africa. The word *matatu* comes from Swahili *ma tatu*, which means "for three." For three Kenyan shillings (during colonial times), one could travel on any route. A *matatu* is a minibus, usually a Nissan, that goes around picking up passengers until they are crammed in like sardines. There is no timetable; you leave for your destination when the driver decides the vehicle is as full as possible—that he has maximized his profits for the trip. A *matatu* is considered full when several people are hanging out the back door and the top is covered with baggage and livestock such as chickens. Once the *matatu* is ready to go, it heads to its destination, where it refills for the return trip. The more trips the *matatu* operator makes, the more money he earns.

I wanted to experience a *matatu* ride. When I arrived at the departure point, only a few people were waiting.

No lineup or queue. After about fifteen minutes, a *matatu* appeared; by this time a crowd had developed, so there was a rush to get into it. Not being used to this, I watched while I was pushed and shoved. Men and women in business suits going to work, university students, and others shoved past me, cutting in line to get into the *matatu*. I attempted to climb into what appeared to be a sea of humanity in a bus meant for approximately nine people.

When the *matatu* was jammed to capacity, the driver decided to leave. I moved to the back, holding my breath against the terrible body odour and sweat exacerbated by the afternoon sun. I bumped into people as I moved, since the driver kept changing gears and jerking his *matatu* to pick up speed as if he was in the East African Safari Rally. I finally got a seat in the back row. People were chatting in languages I couldn't understand—tribal languages, not Swahili. A radio was blaring African songs as if someone could actually appreciate music in this hullabaloo. Not a single Asian or European was on board because they do not use *matatus*. The only Europeans who would ride in one might be youngsters, usually Peace Corps volunteers, who were in the country for the first time. But for me, this was one of my first experiments in local living.

Meanwhile I was adjusting to my new life, but I found the pace at the *Daily Nation* somewhat hectic. I was hired specifically to work on the Sunday edition of the newspaper—the *Sunday Nation*—which had a smaller copy desk. We had a corner newsroom, overlooking an alley, and almost every other day a purse-snatcher would run by, followed by a small crowd shouting, *"Muizi, muizi!"* (Thief, thief!). At first it was a spectacle to watch, and we soon lost interest, but the incidents gave some indication as to the degree of violence in the city and the extent of poverty that existed. Purse-snatchings and bank robberies were both quite common occurrences, displaying the disparities between the people and the fact that some people had to steal to survive. Armed men were bold enough to stage robberies successfully in Nairobi, while such incidents were largely unheard of in Dar es Salaam.

The first thing that struck me when I entered the *Daily Nation* newsroom was that all typewriters were chained either to the ground or to the desks, making it impossible to carry them away. Clearly, even typewriters in an office were not safe from thieves.

About a quarter of the staff in the paper's editorial department were still British expatriates. There were a few Asians in the department, mainly Goans. I happened to be the only Ismaili. It surprised me, as Kenyan Ismailis were proud of the paper; it had been started by the Aga Khan in 1959 as a part of his Nation Media Group, founded to provide a platform for African nationalists who were then fighting for independence. The *Daily Nation* was fully supported by Ismailis as both readers and advertisers. Today, the Nation Media Group is East and Central Africa's largest private media enterprise; in addition to the *Daily Nation*, it also publishes major newspapers in Tanzania (the *Citizen*) and Uganda (the *Daily Monitor*).

All in the Family

WHEN MY YOUNGEST BROTHER, MEB, WAS BORN IN 1958 in Lindi, his four siblings were quite a bit older. The youngest of the elder four was my sister Nasim, who was twelve at the time. Having a baby brother in the house was an exciting and happy occasion. Fashionable ready-made baby clothes were ordered from Dar es Salaam.

My sisters pledged to teach the baby nothing but English words to ensure that he would be fluent in the language. They wanted to make him a modern guy. My brother Shiraz, who was a good athlete, wanted Meb to be an excellent hockey and cricket player like him. He vowed to take his youngest brother under his wing and take him to all his matches so that he (Meb) could understand the games from early childhood.

Nothing was spared for the new baby; he was showered with all kinds of things because he had the love of four older siblings and parents who could now afford to buy him things that we older children had once had to share among us. When we older siblings were growing up, Mom kept some of my older trousers that were in good condition until they would fit my younger brother, and the same thing went for my sisters, but things were different for Meb. He got everything new.

When my parents moved to Dar es Salaam in 1964, Meb's privileged life continued. As a spoiled child, he got whatever he wanted, including a collection of toys and bikes. With his mischievous nature, he and his gang of neighbourhood kids caused havoc in the Ismaili housing complex, City Flats, where my parents lived.

After graduating from Makerere Medical School in Uganda, Shiraz and his wife, Gwen, came to Dar es Salaam's Muhimbili Hospital to do their internships, after which they were posted to Dodoma—Shiraz as district medical officer and Gwen to the Mirembe Psychiatric Hospital. At this time, President Nyerere was going full speed ahead with nationalization, and Asians had started leaving Tanzania. In 1972, Shiraz and Gwen also decided that it may be time for them to think about their future.

Their plan was to first go to Kampala, Uganda. Tanzania was at war with Uganda at the time, because Tanzania had offered political asylum to Uganda's president, Milton Obote. Nyerere was trying to reinstate Obote, who was overthrown in 1971 by Idi Amin. Uganda was, therefore, a safe haven for defectors; after graduation, those educated on government scholarships in Tanzania, like my brother and his wife, were expected to join the government service, and Uganda would not send back those Tanzanians who were breaking the government contract and not serving their country.

No one except one friend knew about their plan to defect to Uganda. Shiraz didn't sleep the whole week before they went. He had visions of being caught in the process. He lost fifteen pounds before they even got started. Since he was the district medical officer, he made up a fictitious file number and typed a letter saying, "Drs. Shiraz and Gwen Ladha have to go to Nairobi to see their relative who is very sick, so please allow them to cross the border." He signed the letter as the officer in charge.

The friend came to my brother's home after work with a taxi, and Shiraz and Gwen were waiting with bags packed. The couple left Dodoma and drove all night to Arusha, where they changed taxis and left for the border. At the Tanzania-Kenya border, the *askari* (policeman) asked

Shiraz the purpose of his visit. Shiraz showed his forged letter; the *askari* read it and found it very official. He wrote down all the details, including the fake file number. Shiraz and Gwen were allowed to cross the Kenyan border.

After a brief rest, they decided to head for Kampala, from where they wouldn't be forced to return to Tanzania. Shiraz had only seventy Kenyan shillings, with which he bought one-way bus tickets to Kampala; relatives there provided the couple with accommodation and helped them in whatever way they could. After a few days, Shiraz and Gwen went to Entebbe—a major town thirty-seven kilometres south of Kampala—to apply for medical licences and jobs with the Uganda Medical Association. Both of them were given jobs in Arua, Idi Amin's hometown, in northern Uganda.

Initially, they stayed at Arua Hotel for a few days. The hotel was full of Israeli engineers and other technicians who had come to Uganda to build an airport for Amin in Arua. One fine evening, to Shiraz's amazement, the hotel was completely empty. Amin, a Muslim, had gone on hajj to Mecca and visited Muammar Gaddafi in Libya before returning home, resulting in a shifting of allegiance. Now, Amin had become vociferously anti-Israel and decided to expel the Israeli ambassador and all Israelis who were in Uganda to build his airport.

In his capacity as the district medical officer, Shiraz had to visit the prison. During his prison visits, my brother came in contact with several of former prime minister Obote's ministers, and a few of them even asked Shiraz to sneak out letters for them. Much as he would have liked to help, he had to be extra careful because military policemen always accompanied him, and he didn't want to get involved. As a government doctor, Shiraz could have met Amin if he'd wanted to, but he purposely maintained a low profile. In his words, although a visible minority, he "tried to become as invisible as possible."

His job also included house calls to the Amin family and physicals for members of Amin's Kakwa tribe. When Shiraz needed to go to the Amin household, a Land Rover was sent to pick him up. He remembers seeing a huge photograph of Queen Elizabeth in the foyer along with a replica of an aircraft with a plaque inscribed, "To Idi Amin Dada." In 1965, Amin had gone to Israel for paratrooper training; though he did not complete the course, he received paratrooper wings because he was an important officer of a country friendly to Israel.

Every time Amin was at a function in Arua, Shiraz was invited. He would attend the function but would ensure that he was not noticeable. You did not want to be noticed in Amin's Uganda. As was very commonly known, the

Owen Falls in Jinja were clogged with fat crocodiles that were well fed by Amin with human corpses. Shiraz's behaviour in Amin's Uganda was appropriate. Anyone who saw the movie *The Last King of Scotland* will likely remember what happened to the Scottish doctor who came too close to Idi Amin. (In the movie, Dr. Nicholas Garrigan, a Scottish doctor on a Ugandan medical mission, becomes irreversibly entangled with Amin. Impressed by Garrigan's brazen attitude in a moment of crisis, Amin handpicks him as his personal physician and closest confidante. Though Garrigan is at first flattered and fascinated by his new position, he soon awakens to Amin's savagery and his own complicity in it. Horror and betrayal ensue as Garrigan tries to right his wrongs and escape Uganda alive. Although Garrigan is a fictional character, the film is based loosely on a true story.)

Things were getting difficult in Uganda. Every morning, someone went missing and his body was later found in the Nile River. After about six months, Shiraz and Gwen decided to leave Uganda. It was time to apply for a visa to the United States. Shiraz was called for an interview in Kampala and, after a few days, he received confirmation of visa approval. Shiraz resigned his position on the pretext of going for further studies. A World Health Organization statistician, with whom he played squash, gave the couple a ride to Entebbe International Airport. On the way, they stopped for lunch at a riverside hotel where, chillingly, they noticed that the crocodiles had apparently gained weight.

Shiraz and Gwen's first stop in the United States was Pittsfield, Massachusetts, where after a brief residency Shiraz was invited to join a group of doctors, while Gwen worked at a veterans hospital in Albany, New York. Later, she specialized in clinical and internal medicine and started a practice in Pittsfield. Along the way, she got a master's degree in public health. The weather eventually enticed Shiraz and Gwen to move to Phoenix, Arizona, where Shiraz has had a thriving pediatrics practice for over twenty-two years. Gwen, now retired, volunteers for several private agencies—work that has included volunteering for an HIV project in Kampala, Uganda.

After he finished standard six, in elementary school, Meb was sent to live with Shiraz and Gwen in Pittsfield, because education in Tanzanian schools was becoming too political with the introduction of Swahili. Meb looked forward to the challenge of living in a Western country, and it was his first time out of his home country. One evening after his arrival, Meb accompanied Shiraz to a friend's house for dinner. The host asked him if he would like some snacks before dinner. Meb, a newcomer to the

United States, was bewildered to hear that people there have "snakes" before dinner. To this day, the host teases Meb about eating snakes.

Gwen, a staunch Catholic, placed Meb in a Catholic school, where he was the only non-Catholic student. While touring the school on his first day, Meb couldn't help but notice that all the students were staring at him. During the lunch break, he was sitting alone when a friendly girl named Susan came up to him and started a conversation. Susan was flabbergasted by seeing a brown-skinned kid—apparently for the first time. "Can I touch your skin?" she asked. "I like its tone." Meb allowed her to touch him, and she later became his girlfriend. With her, Meb was involved in school dances and other extracurricular events. "This was my introduction to life in America," he has said.

Life in Pittsfield was very regimented for Meb, who was given household chores to do. Meb's duty was to load and unload the dishwasher and set the table for dinner. He was allowed to watch TV between five-thirty and six, when he would watch *Hogan's Heroes*. On weekends, TV time was extended by one extra hour. Meb got involved in extracurricular activities and joined the table tennis club. He also became a guest speaker at other schools, talking about his life in Africa and why people of Asian descent were leaving Africa. "Contrary to popular belief, people in Africa are not going around with spears," he told his American audiences.

Studying in a Catholic school meant that every Friday was a confession day. Students would line up to go into the confession booth and confess their sins. His first time, Meb stood in line unaware of what to expect. When his turn came, the priest said, "Welcome, my son. What do you have to confess today?"

"Nothing," Meb replied.

"All humans are sinners. Repent, my son," the priest insisted, while Meb kept emphasizing that he was not a sinner. When he later described the episode to Gwen, she explained the Catholic practice and said that he would just have to go along with the tide.

Meb caught the culinary bug watching Gwen, an excellent cook, prepare various dishes. She would make Indian dishes, using homemade spices and fresh ingredients, on the weekend, and then freeze them for the week. This experience provided Meb with a stepping stone to his future hospitality and restaurant career. He also developed a taste for wine after first drinking it from a sacramental jug in church!

Later, the family moved to Guilderland, New York, where Shiraz and Gwen did their residencies at Pittsfield

General Hospital and Meb, the impressionable kid from Tanzania, enjoyed his time. Meb started school in the middle of a term. He had hardly been in school four weeks when the social studies exam was scheduled. The teacher later told the class that they hadn't done well on the test, adding, "By the way, Meb, you are second-class." Meb thought the teacher meant he'd come second in the whole class, but a classmate told him that that was not what the teacher meant.

When Meb told Shiraz about the incident, Shiraz phoned the school for an explanation. A parent-teacher meeting including the principal was held. The teacher explained that in accordance with policies of South Africa, which was at the time still governed by a racist regime, whites were first-class, coloureds second-class, and blacks third-class—coloureds meaning people with brown skin. According to that classification, Meb was designated a second-class citizen.

Shiraz and Gwen were both shocked to hear this from a teacher in the United States, and so was the principal, who maintained that the teacher's remark had been inappropriate. Shiraz demanded that the teacher be fired for his racist remarks. The process took some time, but Shiraz was adamant that the teacher be taught a lesson in civility and race relations. My brother refused to accept that his coming to the United States was an exercise in futility.

Aftermath of Amin's Order

IN AUGUST 1972, IDI AMIN GAVE ALL ASIANS IN UGANDA ninety days to leave the country. Their property and other wealth was confiscated. Amin stated that he wanted to transfer "economic control of Uganda into the hands of Ugandans." It was a warning to all Asians throughout the rest of East Africa of what could one day happen to them. So, most families made plans to send at least one member, usually a professional, to England, North America, or Europe so that if they had to leave in a hurry, they would have somewhere to go to.

Members of the Asian business community in Tanzania were getting restless and nervous. The scene was set for them, and had been long before Amin expelled the people from Uganda. President Nyerere had gone full speed ahead with his 1967 Arusha Declaration and the policy of *ujamaa* (cooperative economics), or "familyhood," as it was called. The declaration defined the public ownership and nationalization policies of the government clearly, confirming that the president had launched a platform for a socialist society. Under the *ujamaa* policy, villages were to practise collective agriculture, kibbutz-style, and villagers were to live on the collective proceeds.

Nyerere maintained that his socialist policies were not directed towards the Asian business class. However, Asians were the ones who owned buildings, properties, businesses, and farms, and they were directly affected—nationalization's paramount victims. The government offered no compensation when it assumed ownership of their assets, leaving many Asians virtually penniless. The properties, many of which had been rented out, had provided families with retirement income, on which many depended. This was their pension for the future. The socialist government took this future away; subsequently, many Asians didn't see any point in staying in the country.

My father lost a three-storey rental property because he was classified a *mirija*, an "exploiter of the masses," according to the socialist jargon. While the government nationalized his rental property, it did leave him the family's principal residence. This was Nyerere's African socialist justice!

As the owner of a wholesale produce shop, Dad also began to have difficulty getting supplies. His customers began complaining, business declined, and there was an uneasiness in the marketplace due to widespread shortages. Day by day, Nyerere—who was busy translating *Julius Caesar* into Swahili—made it increasingly difficult to earn a living in the business community.

Although the Asians were hated, they had been indispensable to the country's economic development during the colonial period, and still were during reconstruction post-independence. Even before the colonial era, European explorers had depended on the Asians for supplies and credit, although when some of these adventurers returned home they wrote about the Asians as "Shylocks" and in other unflattering terms. And the trend of persecution had continued to the present. Asians in East Africa, among them the Ismailis, were often victims of a regular diet of diatribe in newspapers and radio commentaries, and attacks by government officials.

In Kenya between 1965 and 1967, panic-stricken Asians, fearful that their right to go to Britain would be taken away, began to exercise it. Their annual number of entrants to Britain increased from 6,150 to 13,600. In the first two months of 1968 alone, 12,800 Asians emigrated from Kenya. They left in greater and greater numbers, because they were fearful (and rightly so) that the UK might at any time deprive them of their rights of entry and of residence.[6]

In 1971, Uganda's president Milton Obote was overthrown in a coup led by Idi Amin. Amin was initially accepted by Britain, the first country to recognize his regime; however, Amin's true colours became evident when he expelled the British high commissioner and nationalized British firms. Determined to make Uganda "a black man's country," Amin expelled the country's forty to fifty thousand Indians, Pakistanis, and Ugandan Asians, reportedly after receiving a message from God in a dream. Amin's dream became Uganda Asians' nightmare.

Asians, the majority of whom were third-generation Ugandans, were given ninety days to leave the country and were allowed to take only what they could carry. "If they do not leave, they will find themselves sitting on the fire," Amin warned. The businesses, homes, and possessions Asians left behind were distributed to Amin's military favourites.

"I am going to ask Britain to take responsibility for all Asians in Uganda who are holding British passports, because they are sabotaging the economy of the country," Amin said.

In his book *General Amin*, David Martin, a former colleague of mine at the *Standard* in Dar es Salaam, expounds a bizarre theory that Amin expelled Asians because a widow of an Asian millionaire refused to marry him.[7] Although Amin's actions presented a golden opportunity to presidents Kenyatta of Kenya, Nyerere of Tanzania, and Kaunda of Zambia to send their "brown Britons" to their "homeland," nothing of the sort happened. The trio restrained themselves, to everyone's relief.

But as Martin says, "Amin's blatant racialism and anti-Semitism deeply affected African credibility."[8] The most important cornerstone of the Organization of African Unity (OAU) had been its commitment to the liberation of southern Africa from white minority domination, apartheid, and, importantly, racism; but in the cases of racism in Uganda and the ethnic slaughter in Burundi, African leaders and the OAU, with few exceptions, remained silent.

It was a shameful episode in African history, as many African leaders, usually vocal in their denunciation of racialism, were noticeably quiet about Amin's treatment of his country's Asians. But the international community didn't keep quiet. Outside of Africa, there was an outcry in response to Uganda's forced Asian exodus, the largest in African history.

Amin was an African dictator who could not be trusted, and many Asians in other East African nations wondered if the writing was on the wall. Would other leaders declare, like Amin had done, that they didn't want any brown citizens in their countries? Asians in Tanzania and Kenya feared it could happen. That they could be stripped of their citizenship. That they could also become stateless, like Ugandan Asians. Then what? The thinking was to prepare for the worst.

The atmosphere filled with uncertainty and gloominess. Asians started asking questions: "Where do we go?" "Who will accept us?" "When do we leave?" Many felt the political situations in their countries had deteriorated incredibly in a few short years and were fearful as to what the future would bring. Many began to feel that it was better to leave sooner than later, before they had to do so in a panic.

The situation had become so tense and precarious that even friends didn't inform each other of their plans for fear that someone would leak the information to the authorities, thus hampering or preventing their departure. It was common to hear that one of your friends had suddenly disappeared and gone to the United States or Canada or Britain. Sadly, no one felt they could trust anyone. Stories came out after people had left. Due to fear of the governments' plans, a mini exodus from Tanzania and Kenya began.

Mandatory national service had by now become a reality in Tanzania. Youths, including high school, college, and university students and graduates, regardless of where they were at in their lives, were expected to go to Mgulani Camp to undergo military training. My youngest brother, Meb, the baby of the family and the fifth sibling, who was in grade eight, had to participate. The youngsters slept in tents, woke up at 5:00 a.m. for their military training, did exercises, and ran in the afternoons. It was a three-month course for juniors.

Brigadier Patrick Kongo, the camp commandant, had a voice so loud that some said it was audible as far away as South Africa. He was short in stature, sported a Hitler-like moustache, and was a highly politicized party stalwart. And he would brainwash the boys with his speech: "I am here to instill some sense into you boys and to show you how to love your country and respect its flag. We had to fight to get *uhuru* (freedom.) You must understand that, and therefore you must guard it with vengeance and with your lives. We will show you how to identify the enemies of the country and how to eradicate them."

A graduation ceremony, to which parents were invited, was held on the final day of the camp. My parents couldn't go, so my wife and I substituted for them. We mingled with the crowd and waited for the guest of honour, the regional commissioner, Mr. Songambele, to arrive.

After a while, an announcement was made that Songambele had been held up somewhere, so one of the parents would be chosen as the guest of honour instead. The speaker had hardly finished the sentence when the guy behind me pushed me and said, "Here is the right guy for the occasion." Everyone started clapping. Before I realized what was happening, I was the guest of honour!

I had to march past the graduating class. An army officer with a drawn sword accompanied me while we inspected the guard of honour. When I approached my kid brother I stopped, undid one of his shirt buttons, and asked him, "Soldier, how come one of your buttons is open?" Poor Meb started sweating and fumbled some inaudible words. I closed his button and said, "Make sure next time it's closed properly. Carry on, soldier." As we moved forward, the accompanying officer couldn't resist smiling.

When we approached the platform, I was expected to address the graduates in Swahili. Fortunately for me, my Swahili at the time was not too bad.

So I began: "Ladies, gentlemen, parents, graduating students, and my fellow countrymen, this is an important day in the lives of our young graduating students who have just finished their three months of military training.

National service training is important because it will be useful to defend our country if and when the need arises. We should all be prepared to defend our nation, our independence, our freedom. It is good that our youths have had this training when they are young, so that they can instill the same virtues in their own children when they become parents.

"National service is what your nation demands of you. The country has educated you, and now it is your turn to give back to the country that has invested in your education." I realized I was beginning to sound like President Nyerere addressing the university students. "This graduating class today has demonstrated that they are willing to serve their country by undergoing this training and being ready to serve when called upon to do so. It is the duty of every citizen to guard our nation's sovereignty. We salute them for their dedication and commitment. Now the graduating class will receive their certificates."

The audience liked my brief speech, clapping enthusiastically. I was proud that I could think of what to say on the spur of the moment. Most of all, I wished President Nyerere had been present to hear me—a former "ringleader," as he'd put it, and one of those who supposedly opposed national service—making a plea for youths to go into the service. What an irony! How could I forget the injustice that I had suffered?

Meanwhile, my family had finally decided it was time to leave Tanzania. The choice was to go either to England, Canada, or the United States. My brother Shiraz and his wife, Gwen, were already in the States, as was one of my two sisters; the other was in London, England. They were all well settled with their families. We didn't have to worry about them.

Among us Ismailis, Canada was a desirable English-speaking Commonwealth country to emigrate to, due to the personal friendship of then Canadian prime minister Pierre Trudeau and the Aga Khan, which greatly facilitated Asian East Africans' easy entry into the country.

England, with whom Ismailis and other Asians had close ties because of the recent colonial past, was considered less desirable: it had already absorbed a large "coloured" population from its former colonies, and a mounting and palpable racial animosity existed towards these non-white immigrants. The famous "Rivers of Blood" speech by British Conservative politician Enoch Powell in Birmingham in 1968 had fuelled the racial pyre. In his controversial speech, Powell—who was later sacked from the Conservative shadow cabinet—warned that uncontrolled immigration would change the face of Britain irrevocably.

Thus, I chose Canada over Britain. I also vividly remembered a bitter experience I'd had in 1970 when I was studying journalism in Cardiff. Four other Commonwealth journalists and I had, excitedly but foolishly, gone to Birmingham to cover another one of Powell's speeches for our respective papers. As we came out of the bus station, we were confronted by a group of savage-looking "skinheads," apparently out for some good fun. With chains in their hands they chased us down a crowded street, shouting, "Paki! Paki!"—a word I have always hated and consider worse than the F-word because of the racism it represents.

As soon as we saw a restaurant, we ran in and told the owner what was happening. Bless his soul, he was sympathetic and allowed us to stay until the skinheads got tired of waiting. We finally made our escape through the back door to the bus station to catch the return bus to Cardiff, without covering the Powell speech. That's how explosive the racial and political environment in Britain was against non-white immigrants at the time.

So, being proud as I am, I decided there was no way I would go to Britain—a country that didn't welcome immigrants if they were not white. So I applied for a visa for Canada, for my family of three.

"Canadian Experience"

WHEN MY CANADIAN VISA ARRIVED, I WAS IN MY FIFTH month of a two-year contract with the *Daily Nation* in Nairobi, enjoying life as a socialist turned expatriate. I took a leave of absence from work and took an exploratory trip to Toronto, leaving my wife and son behind. I wanted to find out whether I could get a job with my qualifications and to determine whether I would like the place enough to call it home.

I stayed with a group of Ismailis, most of whom were "bachelors" who were expecting to call their families once they were settled. We lived in an old house where everyone shared the costs of rent, utilities, and food. It was a fun stay, and everyone supported each other.

The group always included people who could provide information on immigration and citizenship, social security, the Canada Pension Plan, and employment insurance. From them, I also learned about the problems immigrants were having in getting jobs in Canada in their professions, and that many immigrants' qualifications were not recognized in the country. I was somewhat disappointed and feared that I might have to drive a cab or clean toilets to make a living.

Nonetheless, during this leave from my job at the *Daily Nation* I decided to test the Canadian job market. Because I had graduated from the Thomson Foundation course in Cardiff, I decided to try my luck at Thomson House on Bay Street. When I graduated, Ken Thomson, a Canadian, had come to the graduation ceremony to present the certificates. At the reception that followed, I had a picture taken of the two of us talking. So, I phoned his office, explaining I was a Fellow from Cardiff Thomson Journalism School, and I wanted to pay a courtesy call to Mr. Thomson. The secretary passed on the message to Thomson, and I was given an appointment for the following week.

When I arrived, I was escorted to Thomson's private office, and he was very cordial. I showed him our photograph, and we chatted about the Thomson Foundation course and my time in Cardiff. I told him that I was in Toronto with my landed immigrant papers, intending to settle in Canada.

"We always like to help our Thomson Fellows," Thomson responded—to my amazement—and he picked up the phone and summoned one of his officials. The gentleman was asked to help me. I shook hands with Thomson and said goodbye.

The official took my resume, and the following week I received a call informing me that he had a job for me with the *Sudbury Star*. He was wondering when I would be prepared to start. I was very anxious to start a job and gain some experience, so in two days' time I left Toronto to start my first job with a Canadian newspaper. In Sudbury, 1972 was a historic year: U.S. astronauts were there at the time, practising on the nickel mining area's landscape, which somewhat resembled the moon. However, I was disappointed that I was made the paper's court reporter. At East African newspapers, court reporting duties were given to entry-level applicants to test their understanding of legal proceedings and their ability to report. Here in Canada, with six years of senior editorial experience as a copy and features editor, I was only considered good enough to be a court reporter at a newspaper—and in Sudbury!

So, day by day, I was getting frustrated on the job, and I was lonely because I was without my family and had no friends. People at the paper made no attempts to be friendly, and the work did not meet my expectations.

On my way to Canada, a friend in London, Zubeda Bhagat, had given me her sister and brother-in-law's phone number. She said they lived in a small mining town in Ontario. I took the number, thinking my chances of ever going to this godforsaken place were slim. But then, while in Sudbury, I was studying a map of Ontario and saw that this town—Elliot Lake—was very close. So I gave them a call, and they invited me to spend the weekend. And it was in Elliot Lake that I was introduced to my first Canadian custom: taking off your winter boots at the entrance to a home when you visit. My newfound friends, Kurban and Gulshan Keshvani, were very hospitable. They now live in Vancouver, and we have remained good friends since our first meeting.

After about a month on the job back in Sudbury, I resigned and went back to Nairobi. Soon after my return, the Asian exodus from Uganda began to take place, and everyone in Kenya was telling me how foolish I had been to return when I had already been in Canada, and with a job. The job had definitely not been to my liking, but I could have stayed and looked for a better one. I soon realized my foolishness.

My wife and I decided to leave Nairobi permanently after living there less than a year; I took my family back to our new home in Canada in December 1972. We were among thousands of Asians forced out of African countries simply for being what we were—African-born, but of Asian ancestry.

As our plane approached Toronto, we could see fields and farms, tiny homes, and, as we got closer, the skyscrapers so familiar in the city's skyline, and its superhighways. It was a cold wintry day when our flight landed in Toronto. From the air, the land was blanketed with white snow as far as one could see.

"Welcome to Canada," a huge sign at the entrance to the immigration queue said. There were about ten lineups of passengers, as several flights had arrived. Toronto was the favourite entry point of immigrants to the country.

* * *

When we arrived in Toronto, it was difficult to settle down without any help from friends or relatives. Imagine having to find a home in a new and strange city and country within a day. It was difficult to leave belongings, relatives, friends, home and familiar surroundings, and arrive with meagre funds and everything squeezed in a suitcase. The financial loss for us was enormous, but the emotional one was incalculable. We arrived in with only $1,000 with which to make our fresh start, but we had high hopes.

Adjusting to life in Canada was not easy. We had come from a society that relied on servants, where *yes Bwana* (yes sir) and *yes Mama* (yes madam) was the order of the day. In Dar, our servant Juma doubled as a cook, while our son had a full-time nanny, Yasintah. As a senior staff member with the *Standard*, I had the privilege of residing in a company-provided, fully furnished two-bedroom flat right in front of the Indian Ocean in a Europeans-only area—one of the fruits of *uhuru* that we formerly colonized folks had received.

In Africa, meals were always ready for *memsahib* (madam), and baby Hanif was pampered from birth, till we left Dar es Salaam, by our indispensable, ever-present nanny. When Hanif did his first "big job" in Toronto, we didn't know what to do, as we had never performed this "operation"; Anaar and I tossed a coin to determine who was going to clean him! In Canada, my wife became the breadwinner, reversing the traditional role. Washing dishes, cleaning the house, and picking up and dropping off Hanif at the daycare became my chores as the househusband. Unlike my two brothers, who have become excellent cooks, I was lost in the kitchen and had an extreme dislike of doing anything other than making tea or toast or boiling an egg.

I recall our first Christmas in Canada in 1973. On one stormy, snowy, wintry night, I was looking out my front window. I could see the snow blowing on the empty street before me. Our street, called Christmas Lane, was adorned with bright-coloured lights and decorations.

Every year in the middle of November, our neighbour Greg—dubbed the "self-styled Santa"—eagerly took it upon himself to remind everyone on the street that it was time to decorate for the festive season. He didn't care about the mounting power bills, or that some seniors couldn't afford to light up so early, or that some of us were Muslims and so Christmas had no religious significance to us.

"When in Rome, do as the Romans do," I told my family. So, in the spirit of good neighbourliness and Christmas, I would religiously—no pun intended—decorate our home. For the sake of our two-year-old son that first year, we decided to have a Christmas tree. We wanted to reflect the true Canadian spirit and tradition. However, some friends were outraged upon hearing that I, a true Muslim, was going to put a Christmas tree in my house. "This is not in our religion or our belief!" they argued.

"A Christmas tree has nothing to do with religion" was my reply. "We are now in Canada, and we should live and adopt a Canadian way of life, but that doesn't mean we have to forget our religion and culture." This didn't satisfy them, but to each their own.

During those early days in Canada, our community of new immigrants from East Africa grew and everyone enjoyed going to *jamatkhana*s (Ismaili prayer houses), which were being held in school gymnasiums, mainly because we didn't have permanent facilities then. Every Friday, one would meet new families and individuals who had arrived the previous week from either Kenya or Tanzania, and it could be one's relative, a friend, or someone else we knew. The *jamatkhana* became a drop-in and networking centre for all Toronto-area Ismailis.

Ismaili volunteers would go early to the *jamatkhana*s to lay carpets for the congregation to sit on, with legs crossed to pray. Many didn't even have jobs at the time, but volunteerism was in their blood and they would come to *jamatkhana* to donate their services.

Many people who couldn't get jobs in their professions, because they lacked "Canadian experience," became insurance or real estate agents; they found *jamatkhana*s the best places to ply their trade. With the captive audience there, one could collect at least five business cards each week.

As time went on, places like Toronto, Vancouver, Calgary, and Edmonton established permanent *jamatkhana*s, and it became quite common to ask people which *jamatkhana* they attended. The answer was like a postal code or a trademark—whether one was from the Belle Rive *jamatkhana* in Edmonton, or Northwest *jamatkhana* in Calgary, or Burnaby *jamatkhana* near Vancouver, or Willowdale *jamatkhana* near Toronto. Even today, Ismailis identify themselves not by the area they live in, but by the *jamatkhana* they attend.

I had arrived in Toronto armed with seven years of senior editorial experience and British journalism training, thinking that getting a job would be easy. I was wrong. On the recommendation of a high-profile individual, I went to see the managing editor of one of the Toronto newspapers. Instead of looking at my resume, he chastised me for having not only the aspiration but the audacity to seek a job at one of the major newspapers in Canada. He suggested that I should work on "one of the smaller weeklies" to start because I didn't have "Canadian experience." I was shocked to hear this. My experience and training were considered worthless. I thought newspapers were liberal, progressive institutions. I threw him a challenge. Granted, I lacked so-called Canadian experience (whatever that meant), but I was prepared to work for a month free of charge as a copy editor; after one month, if he wasn't happy with me, all he had to do was tell me to go away and I wouldn't question his decision. I told him what I had was journalism experience: copy editing and layout skills were universal, and I had been doing that work on

English-language newspapers in Dar es Salaam and Nairobi. I was confident that I could do the job. So I begged this editor to at least give me a chance.

As an aside, this particular paper had recently hired a British colleague of mine, who had also been a copy editor at the *Daily Nation* in Nairobi, without any Canadian experience! I'd had lunch with the guy the previous day, and I used that information as my trump card. I asked, "How come my white former colleague from Africa was hired without any Canadian experience?" There was complete silence in the room. Needless to say, I didn't get the job. Fortunately, my wife was hired as a secretary with Bell Canada one week after our arrival, so we had one income. Someone at Bell Canada took the chance to hire her based on her experience as a senior administrative secretary—despite the fact that she didn't have "Canadian experience."

Every immigrant of colour, when seeking a job in Canada, has been asked at least once whether he or she has had Canadian experience. It used to be a standard question in an interview, and it presents a conundrum that many thousands of newcomers must face each year. This Canadian experience requirement was first cited as a barrier for new immigrants to access jobs as early as the 1970s, and it was, and remains, a Catch-22 situation. No Canadian experience, no job. No job, no Canadian experience.

The problem became so acute that in 2013 the Ontario Human Rights Commission (OHRC) was forced to launch a new policy directive denouncing the requirement for so-called Canadian experience as discriminatory. OHRC Chief Commissioner Barbara Hall stated that the new policy "can help remove these barriers and give employers and regulatory bodies the tools they need to respect human rights. The starting point . . . is a simple one: insisting on Canadian experience is discrimination under the Human Rights Code."

Today, the law requires that employers and professional regulatory bodies not exclude anyone based on race, ancestry, colour, place of origin, or ethnic origin. However, in practice, some employers still demand Canadian experience as a prerequisite to employment, and as a result many skilled people are still prevented from effectively participating in the workforce.

It was particularly ironic that the Canadian experience rule was applied to Asians from East Africa, because theirs was a dynamic community with Western education and Western liberal values that were consistent with Canadian values. Additionally, some of these immigrants—being professionals and people with achievements in law, business, sciences, and the arts—could have made great contributions to the country. Unfortunately, many never realized their potential in Canada because of the quandary over Canadian experience.

In their desperate search for work, some people even anglicized their names. They believed that because their names were easily recognizable as being "foreign," their job applications were immediately placed at the bottom of the pile. So Badru Kanji changed his name to Bud Kanji, Sadru became Sam, Firoz became Phil, Kamru changed his name to Ken, and so on. In our group, there was a guy whose name was Fakroo; jokingly, people would dare him to change his name to something that would sound like the F-word and "you." The poor guy just left his name untouched. I also kept mine, but I did begin to wonder if employers were using the Canadian experience requirement as an excuse to bar non-white immigrants from jobs.

In my own search for work, my strategy was to go to the Greyhound bus depot every morning (since I didn't own a car then), pick and go to an Ontario city, and present myself to the managing editor of the local newspaper. Most of the time I would succeed in seeing the ME or the editor; I would give them my resume and indicate that I was available immediately. Using this strategy, I saw managing editors in London, Kitchener, Waterloo, Guelph, Windsor, and Peterborough, in addition to those at the major Metro Toronto weeklies. I was willing to go anyplace I could find a job. I had written off the Toronto dailies, as they were unashamedly looking for someone with "Canadian experience."

I finally got a break, however, when I went to the Toronto head office of Southam newspapers, a company that owned thirteen major dailies across Canada. The guy in charge was a pleasant young Jewish fellow who was quite sympathetic to my plight. I think he realized that we new Asian immigrants, who were often called the "Jews of East Africa" because of our dominance in trade and commerce, were also a persecuted and "homeless" people. He granted me an interview and sent my resume to a few Southam papers. I heard from two of them right away: Edmonton and Winnipeg, both of which offered me positions as a copy editor. I chose Edmonton, as I would be paid one hundred dollars more per month there than in Winnipeg! One hundred dollars more to a new immigrant making a fresh start was a lot of money. And that's how I ended up at the *Edmonton Journal* in March 1973.

* * *

Friends in Toronto had warned me about harsh Edmonton winters. My response: "I would rather live like a king in Edmonton, where I have a job to go to, than like a beggar in Toronto, where I don't have a job." Soon we found out how right they were—our first winter in Edmonton was terrible. We had snow boots and bundled ourselves up, but we had not yet learned how to walk in the snow and on the city's icy streets. I must have fallen at least three times before I learned the technique of balancing myself in slippery conditions. And the cold temperatures—colder even than Toronto—were something else to get used to.

As I settled into my new life, I found that working on a Canadian daily had its ups and downs. With my previous experience on two English-language dailies, I had no problem working on the copy desk, and I got used to the system in no time. Editing is a universal occupation, whether you practise it in Mumbai, Toronto, or Timbuktu. However, I could sense some hidden animosity towards the paper's non-white staff. Some people were very friendly, but some were not so friendly. One had to tread skilfully between them. One of the reporters bluntly questioned how I, being a non-white whose mother tongue was not English, was capable of editing his stories. He completely ignored the fact that I had done the same thing in my previous jobs. Someone else in the office suggested that they would prefer to call me Mike, but I flatly refused, pointing out that the names of several other staff sounded foreign to me, but I wouldn't suggest they change them to Abdul or Mohamed. I put my foot down, and my colleagues at the paper got used to calling me by name in no time.

As newcomers, Anaar and I wanted to make friends, so we arranged a rice and curry party at our place and invited most of my colleagues from the desk, hoping that someone would at least reciprocate the gesture at some point. Sadly, the reciprocal protocol was overlooked.

However, as I said, there were people who were friendly. One of the guys at the paper offered to find an apartment for me since I didn't know the different areas of the city. He phoned a few places and set up appointments. But when I went to see the places I was told, to my astonishment, that the apartments had been rented. It became obvious that these landlords didn't want to rent them to a brown person. After a few such incidents, I was finally able to get a nice two-bedroom apartment that was to our liking, in an excellent neighbourhood, close to a daycare centre and a bus stop.

In East Africa, most of us were used to buying things with cash. The use of credit cards was not common then. I bought a used black-and-white TV in Edmonton from a priest who was, ironically, going to a Third World assignment, and with my first Visa card, I was able to purchase furniture and appliances from one of the local department stores.

While still a newcomer to the city, I had the privilege of being appointed chairman of the Edmonton Shia Ismaili Muslim community, followers of His Highness the Aga Khan. This appointment was considered quite prestigious, since it came directly from the Aga Khan. In this capacity, I had to oversee the settlement of Ugandan refugees who had just arrived (six thousand had come to Canada) as well as look after the general welfare of other members of the community—responsibilities that placed a strain on my personal life as a new immigrant, himself trying to get settled. However, with the help and dedication of other members of my committee, I was able to discharge my duties successfully for seven years. The crowning glory of my term came when the Aga Khan paid his first visit to Edmonton in 1978, which my wife and I had the privilege to host. I was pleasantly surprised that the Aga Khan vividly remembered the interview I had conducted with him in Dar es Salaam in 1970. I reminded him that I had asked him whether or not Princess Zehra could become imam of the Ismailis in absence of a male heir. He looked at me with a smile on his face and responded, "I remember the interview very well. You were very kind to me."

In 1974, I sponsored my parents' emigration to Canada. A few months after arriving in Edmonton, Dad got bored sitting at home, watching soap operas every afternoon;

unbeknown to me, he found a job at a hospital parking lot. He enjoyed his work as it gave him the chance to meet a lot of people. His workplace was in a built-in cubicle, which kept him safe from the elements. There was also a phone in it, so he could talk to Mom during slack periods. He missed East African life and talked about it periodically, reminiscing about the good old days. However, like others of his generation, he had adjusted very well to the new life in Canada. On Saturday afternoons, a bunch of East African friends would gather at King Eddie, a famous hotel in downtown Edmonton, now demolished, to exchange weekly news over beer and chicken wings. This had become their weekly ritual—Saturday was King Eddie Day!

As far as my career was concerned, in the back of my mind I always knew I wanted to own my own weekly newspaper. As such, I wanted to gain experience working on a weekly, and in 1976 I was hired as associate editor of the *Bonnyville Nouvelle*, a long-established weekly in northeastern Alberta that was published every Monday. Shortly after I started with the paper, Imperial Oil announced that it was investing two billion dollars in a heavy oil project in nearby Cold Lake. This was a huge story for the region, foretelling of boom times, and I was able to publish a special mid-week edition of the paper with details about the project on the afternoon of the announcement. The reaction in the area was astonishing. Readers had not seen anything like this before. The *Nouvelle* received quite a few complimentary phone calls and messages, and the paper became more popular; without any modesty, under my supervision and with my daily newspaper experience, the paper continued to gain prestige due to increased editorial excellence in its coverage.

I had gone to Bonnyville alone, leaving my family in Edmonton for a few months, to determine if I liked the job and the town. I had rented a basement suite with kitchen, living, and bathroom facilities, from an elderly Ukrainian couple. The Romanchuks were kind and religious, and despite having been in Canada for a number of years, both spoke broken English.

My arrangement with them was just as a renter, but they insisted on my having dinner with them when I came home from work. At first I objected, insisting that it was inappropriate for me to dine with them every day, but after a few days I accepted their generosity. After a while, Mr. Romanchuk noticed I had beer in my fridge, and whenever I had a beer before dinner, he would come down to my suite and join me—he was not allowed to drink beer upstairs in his own house. I enjoyed his company and the way he communicated with me in his broken English, with his thick Ukrainian accent. I stayed with the Romanchuks for about four months before my family came to join me in Bonnyville, and during that time I was fed fresh vegetables from Mrs. Romanchuk's garden and cultivated a taste for borscht, kubasa, dumplings, and perogies. It was an excellent introduction to rural hospitality and people.

As I had not worked on a weekly before, the Bonnyville job provided me with excellent training and preparation for my life's ambition of buying my own paper, which I was able to do in 1979. I got my wish when two papers came on the market: the *Airdrie Echo* and the *Morinville Mirror*, both within commuting distance from Calgary and Edmonton, respectively.

Our first choice was the *Airdrie Echo* since it was bigger and more established. My wife also had relatives in Calgary. We put in an offer right at the asking price and the offer was accepted. But unfortunately, while the lawyers were drawing up documents, a better offer, above the asking price, was placed on the table; the result was that the seller's lawyer found a loophole to get out of our contract, and we lost the Airdrie deal.

We went after our second choice, the *Morinville Mirror*, which was losing money at the time, and despite our accountant's objections, we bought it. If we hadn't bought the paper, its previous owners were ready to shut it down. But I had full confidence in myself—that I would turn it around and make it into a professionally produced, readable product. The paper, I am ashamed to admit, was a rag. It was located in a mobile home, on a side street in town, with no signage outside. I didn't like the location from the beginning, so after a few months I found office space on the town's main street and we moved. We mounted a neon sign to announce our presence in the community, proudly trumpeting, "*The Mirror*, your community newspaper."

In just a few weeks, the business community saw a difference in the product and began to support it by advertising with us instead of in the two existing competitors, from St. Albert and Westlock, both of which circulated their papers for free in our area. Another strategy we adopted was to hire an advertising salesperson with instructions to make calls to Edmonton businesses in the western and northern parts of the city, where our readers were likely to shop. This was very appealing to these advertisers, as our paper serviced most suburban commuting towns and villages throughout Sturgeon County, a large trading area north of Edmonton. Apart from Morinville, our newspaper circulated in Legal, Gibbons, Bon Accord, Riviere Qui Barre, rural St. Albert, Redwater, Thorhild, Lamont, Fort Saskatchewan, and Bruderheim. Edmonton Garrison, the Canadian Forces base, was also in Sturgeon County. CFB Edmonton was considered a town in itself, with close to five thousand military personnel and their families, an attractive and lucrative market for Edmonton merchants. In addition to our advertising salesperson, we also employed two full-time reporters and production, layout, and front office staff.

The tables were turned now. As an employer, I was hiring people, and I remembered my early days in Canada when I was not hired because I didn't have "Canadian experience." Many times I felt like asking applicants, just for the fun of it, if they had Canadian experience—especially since the majority of them were straight out of college or university and hadn't any work experience whatsoever—but I never succumbed to the temptation. I hired them solely on their qualification in journalism.

When I took over the newspaper in Morinville, one of my competitors, who had long held a virtual monopoly in the area, didn't like it at all. He felt threatened by a newcomer, especially one belonging to an ethnic community. He told one of the local advertisers, "I give this Paki six months and he'll be out of here!" When the advertiser gave me his message, I told him to deliver my response to the competitor: "Tell him he doesn't know this Paki! Tell him this Paki is here to stay and I'll show him." This Paki bought one paper, started another paper in a different town, and published the two newspapers successfully for twenty-five years. Unfortunately for my competitor, his prophecy didn't come true.

In 1980, a year after we bought the *Mirror*, we established the *Redwater Tribune*, a weekly newspaper serving the northeastern part of Sturgeon County. The going wasn't easy. We were operating in one of the most competitive markets in Alberta, and our competitors used every trick in the book to try to drive us out of business. They offered incentives to advertisers and used every gimmick they could think of, but we ploughed ahead, determined to succeed.

Every Christmas I would book a local restaurant and invite my staff and their families for a Christmas dinner. I could have got out of this practice with the excuse that Christmas had no religious significance to me as a Muslim, but I didn't. For the most part, we would have an enjoyable evening, but once in a while, perhaps after a few drinks, someone would find the courage to ask questions such as "When are we going to get a raise?" or bring up personal or staff-related issues that were confidential. I grew to expect this kind of thing and very quickly learned how to overcome such eventualities and not be sensitive about them.

When I worked as an employee, I always gave a present to my immediate boss at Christmastime. As an employer, I received only one—from Wayne, the advertising manager—even though our staff of eleven expected a Christmas party from me.

Wayne was the longest-serving member of our staff. He was quite a character—a funny but loyal person. I always joked that Hollywood would be well advised to produce a movie on the *Morinville Mirror*, because quite a few characters worked there over a number of years. I would say that they would have to give Wayne's role to Jerry Lewis, and mine to Ed Asner, because I liked to think of myself as a tough no-nonsense news director like Lou Grant on *The Mary Tyler Moore Show*.

Despite being the longest-serving member of the staff, Wayne always addressed me and my wife as Mr. Ladha and Mrs. Ladha, unlike the other staff members, who called us by our first names. Not that we cared, but it said something about Wayne's upbringing, which we appreciated.

We liked to think of our staff as our family, and we treated them as such. In addition to our Christmas parties, my wife would cook Indian food on Sundays, and it was customary for her to send a plate of *pillau* or *biryani* or chicken curry to our staff reporters or typesetter—most of whom were single.

As an employer, however, I occasionally had a difficult task to perform—that of firing an employee. We were not big enough to have human resources personnel, so the burden usually fell on me. Very fortunately, such occasions were few.

As I mentioned, several neighbouring towns in our region distributed their papers in Morinville. One operated in direct competition. It lasted for five years. Another one came some years later. Papers from St. Albert and Westlock, two other towns in the vicinity, sent their reporters to cover council and school board meetings, and their ad salespeople made calls to town businesses. All these competitors also had a habit of enticing our staff with lucrative incentives—but sometimes reporters left even if offered only a tiny increase in wages. As a small community newspaper, we were at the mercy of economic realities. Whenever one of our staff left, it put us behind by three or four months because it took time to advertise the vacancy and to train new employees until they were competent and familiar with local politics. We hired reporters from leading journalism schools, which at the time included Ryerson in Toronto, Carleton in Ottawa, King's College in Halifax, the University of Regina, Edmonton's MacEwan University, and Mount Royal and SAIT in Calgary.

One time, we hired a typesetter from Edmonton who didn't have a car and didn't drive. My son went to Edmonton, twenty-five kilometres away, to pick her up for an interview. We found her an apartment in town and helped her move. One Sunday afternoon, I came to the office, as was my usual practice, and found a note attached to my office door: "I have gone to look for greener pastures. Thanks for employing me for seven years." No notice, no warning. I almost had a heart attack because both the papers had to go to press the next day: you can't put the papers to bed without a typesetter. Fortunately for me, another publishing company came to the rescue and sent their typesetter to help out, and the papers were published and circulated as usual. Later I found out that she had gone to one of our competitors.

As a weekly newspaper publisher, I was on duty twenty-four hours a day, seven days a week. One doesn't realize the demands that are placed on a weekly newspaper publisher. Newspapers are the lifeblood of rural communities. The big daily papers won't cover the local 4-H Club or Lions Club meetings, and they won't go to the local town or county council or Chamber of Commerce or school board meetings unless there's a controversy, whereas the community news reporters will write about average people doing ordinary things that are important to their particular communities. Weeklies are recorders of people's achievements and disappointments, their weddings and deaths. They act as historical documents for the community. As I soon found out, weekly newspapers become products of the publishers' blood, sweat, and tears, because they put all they have into the papers around the clock to make them a success—a labour of love.

On the day the paper was distributed, I would be in the office at 5:00 a.m., helping part-timers who came to stuff flyers into the paper and ensuring that the papers were sent out on time. But usually my day started at 7:30 a.m., and although it officially ended at 6:30 p.m., when I went home for dinner, people would still call me. Although taking photographs was not my duty, I used to get calls from service clubs such as the Lions Club or the Rotary Club to come and take pictures when they had forgotten to call the office earlier. I just couldn't say no, because that was part of the community service a weekly newspaper provided.

Although the hours were long and the work was hard, I did enjoy some fringe benefits of being a newspaper publisher. Once I was returning from the neighbouring town of Gibbons after picking up advertising from the town office. As I was climbing a hill just outside the town, an oncoming police car made a U-turn and came up behind me. The policeman informed me that I had been speeding. I gave him my licence and registration documents, which indicated that the car was registered to the newspaper.

After going through my papers, the policeman said, "Sir, are you the publisher of the *Morinville Mirror*?"

"Yes, I am," I responded.

To my amazement, he said with a smile, "I cannot give a ticket to my hometown publisher."

"I agree with you 100 percent, officer!" I said, smiling and shaking his hand. He let me go.

Anaar and I were also always invited to opening nights at Edmonton's two famous theatres—the Citadel and the Mayfield Dinner Theatre. Both theatres would send us complimentary tickets. The plays at the Citadel were followed by receptions and hors d'oeuvres, while the Mayfield's renowned dinner theatre offered a closed-door private reception with the actors, most of whom were stars of famous TV series such as *Dallas*. Even today, we still miss this glamorous and pampered period of our lives.

While in Morinville, I got involved in the Chamber of Commerce. The Chamber held luncheon meetings every month, and I soon discovered that the business community wanted every notice related to Chamber business to be published free of charge. They hadn't realized that a newspaper was also a business, with staff and other operating expenses like any other commercial enterprise. I put my foot down and started charging them for Chamber notices. I had to explain to them that stories generated from the meetings would be published in the paper free of charge, like any other news, but that all Chamber announcements would be chargeable. After a while the Chamber executive saw where I was coming from, and they accepted it.

In my eagerness to participate in the affairs of the town, I became a director on the executive board and was later appointed to the town's economic board, whose mandate was to promote economic development of the region. Several newsworthy projects were discussed, but I had to keep quiet and not publish any details until the board was ready to announce them publicly. This was hard to do, but I maintained my oath of secrecy as was my duty as a board member. However, when five businesses closed down in town in one month it was a visible sign of the downturn of the local economy, and one of my reporters wrote a story about it, interviewing the owners of the closed stores. I ran their interviews on the front page. At the next economic board meeting, I was chastised for running the story. To my utter amazement, a member of the board told me that it was my duty as a board member not to run stories that were "uncomplimentary" to the town. I couldn't believe it.

I said to the board, "My friends, during my tenure on the board, I have acted as a member of this board first and newspaper publisher second. Five businesses have closed down in this town in one month, which is a major story for any newspaper. Everyone knows about it, as there are five vacancies on the main street of this town. No one can hide them. These are economic realities of the time. What is this board going to do about it? That's what we should be discussing and not why I ran the story.

"The board is being an ostrich and putting its head in the sand. I don't have to explain to anyone why I ran the story, because the board is incapable of comprehending it. I am publishing a newspaper, not a propaganda machine for the Chamber," I said angrily and walked out of the meeting. Next day, I sent in my resignation. But this was only one chapter in our otherwise fulfilling and productive life in the community.

* * *

When I look back at our years in Morinville, I see a thirty-six-year-old man courageously and confidently walking into a largely French-speaking town in 1979, not knowing anyone and investing all of his life's savings into buying a losing business. I also see a foolish young, non-white man trying to establish himself in a predominantly white community whose acceptance of other cultures might have been questionable. As soon as it became known that I had purchased the paper, it was brought to my attention that my ancestry and race were being questioned in "certain quarters." The editor at the time told me that some residents in town were not happy that "an East Indian" had bought the paper. I told him they would have to give me a chance and see for themselves what I was like instead of making a stereotypical judgment. And I'm glad to say the "East Indian" performed well for a quarter century, mostly to everyone's satisfaction. I do recall, however, one ugly incident when a ten-year-old boy entered the front office and started shouting "Paki! Paki!" before running away. Be that as it may, fortunately the majority of the people in the community received us well and began to get to know us.

I concentrated on publishing a better paper than the community had had and doing the best I could. The result was that the *Mirror* started winning awards. Over the years we won awards for best editorial, best local story, best picture, best feature story, and so on, gaining prestige as one of the finest papers in the region. I was proud that despite being in one of the toughest competitive markets, we survived and made progress.

Some of the proudest moments of my career were when, over a period of several years, I attended annual national or provincial conventions of publishers with the distinction of being the only non-white publisher of a mainstream weekly. False modesty aside, I felt like I was an ambassador, carrying the torch for all visible minorities. It made me feel proud, and I would have liked my son to have gone on to become a publisher, but he followed a different career, on a successful path in the oil industry. We were proud to see Hanif graduate from an executive MBA program at Western University in London, Ontario, and his meteoric rise in his career was impressive. He rose to become a company director and a regional manager; currently, he is a successful entrepreneur.

After twenty-five years in Morinville, we received an offer in May 2005 that we couldn't refuse. The Sun Media subsidiary Bowes Publishers—Canada's second-largest publishing group—wanted to buy our two weeklies. As publisher and editor of the *Morinville Mirror* and the *Redwater Tribune*, I had come to believe that the papers needed the economic muscle of a chain to take them to their next level of growth and advancement, and that the weekly newspaper industry had reached a stage where it was going to be difficult, if not impossible, for independent publishers like myself to operate. Anaar and I accepted the offer.

In my last column, a farewell editorial to the readers, I wrote, "No more headlines and deadlines for me! Farewell, so long, dear readers, this is my last day as publisher of both these newspapers after toiling for almost 25 years.

The *Mirror/Tribune* has been sold to Bowes Publishers Ltd., a leading group of weekly newspaper publishers affiliated to Sun Media. They take over June 1, 2005. That means today."

I thanked the area residents, and my gratitude particularly went to our loyal advertisers who had stood by us despite constant attractive offers by the competition. "I salute their loyalty and will always remember their friendship," I wrote in my column.

I also thanked all town councils in the area, the two school boards, and the county council for their continuous support. Some of my editorials had not been welcome in some council chambers over the years, but there were also some that had brought smiles to many councillors' faces.

"I am leaving satisfied and proud that my job here is done," I wrote, "and that the two newspapers have achieved a remarkable standard of excellence in journalism as far as weekly newspapers are concerned. With limited resources, two to three competitors always hounding us, we were able to maintain our standard and win a few provincial awards for editorial excellence along the way.

"Those reporters who have had the privilege of going through the tough Ladha School of Journalism will testify today they have had excellent training," I joked. "Some of them today are working in daily newspapers and television stations across Canada, and I am proud to say that their initial training was in small town Morinville under yours truly, originally from primitive Africa!"

I added that the staff that I left behind, both permanent and part-time, were solid and reliable. There were people who had been with us for five to ten years, and they demonstrated a type of loyalty that doesn't come easy. I said it was going to be hard for us to leave such employees and customers, who had practically become family members. "We are bound to miss them."

But it was time for us to say our goodbyes. I wished the papers and their new owner best wishes for a bright future. "It was nice knowing all of you. From Anaar and Mansoor Ladha. So long, au revoir!" I concluded.

* * *

After we sold the papers in 2005, we moved to Calgary and I went for an interview as a part-time copy editor at the *Calgary Herald*. During the interview, I told the editor that one of my former reporters was a key business writer with the paper. After our meeting, he took me to meet the reporter. I had been quite tough on him when he worked for me. After exchanging pleasantries, the reporter told the news editor, "I am grateful to this man. Everything I know today is because of him." What a testimonial! I had always considered journalism as a covenant and sacred trust with readers. I was tough on my staff who had to produce our stories, but I hoped I was fair in my treatment, thus producing good and well-rounded reporters. I don't know if it was because of the reporter's remarks or due to my experience, but I got the job at the *Calgary Herald* as a copy editor.

The *Herald* was a good paper to work for, with friendly and obliging staff, but we copy editors would start work at 3:00 p.m. and end our shift at 10:00 p.m. after putting the paper to bed. I discovered I just couldn't handle those hours: by the time I came home, it was almost midnight when I settled down to go to sleep. So I ended up tendering my resignation, which was reluctantly, but graciously, accepted by the news editor.

After retiring from active newspaper work after forty-nine years, which included running the two weeklies for twenty-five years, I had pretty much run out of steam. But not quite entirely. I ventured into writing non-fiction, publishing my first book, *A Portrait in Pluralism: Aga Khan's Shia Ismaili Muslims*, in 2008. I have led a life of semi-retirement, freelancing for several newspapers, including the *Calgary Herald* and the *Vancouver Sun*, as well as a number of weeklies. I guess journalism is in my blood.

* * *

I'll never forget Friday the thirteenth in March 2009. I received a phone call that the newspapers I had published for twenty-five years had printed their last editions. Covering almost half a page in big, bold letters, the front pages of both the *Mirror* and the *Tribune* said, "Sorry, We're CLOSED!" It was as if the foreman in the pressroom had shouted, "Stop the presses!" I couldn't believe it.

These two suburban weeklies on the outskirts of Edmonton—the *Morinville Mirror* and the *Redwater Tribune*, which I had purchased as one-year-old "babies" and had brought to maturity until they became full-fledged newspapers attractive enough to be bought by Sun Media, Canada's second-largest newspaper group—were gone. My labour of sweat, hope, and love had fallen victim to the current grim economic reality. Announcing the closure to the stunned communities, Sun Media blamed "increasing economic challenges in the newspaper industry, shrinking advertising revenues and rising costs."

The carnage in the industry had started with the dailies a few months earlier. Every major newspaper in Canada had announced significant layoffs, and the *Halifax Daily News* had folded. In the United States, the *Rocky Mountain News*, Denver's second newspaper, closed abruptly in February, and there were doubts as to whether Seattle's *Post-Intelligencer* would be able to continue to publish unless it could find a suitable buyer. Other U.S. newspapers were also on shaky ground. By the end of the decade, at least a dozen metropolitan dailies had closed in the States. More recently, in Canada, the *Nanaimo Daily News* closed after forty-one years in business, while the *Guelph Mercury*, established in 1867, ceased publishing in January 2016.

Whatever people may say about the death of newspapers in our society, the discussion often obscures the fact that, as a popular commodity, news has a special place with people. Newspapers play a vital role in society, especially in communities like Morinville and Redwater. A city has alternative media like television to cover the news, but in smaller towns it is only the community newspaper that covers local news, town council and school board meetings, local sports, deaths, and weddings—it often is the singular faithful recorder of a community's history.

My wife and I had left our papers in an excellent economic condition, but sadly we had to accept that times change, that even corporate ownership couldn't save them. We lamented the demise of the papers and felt particularly bad for the communities. Both had been a big part of our lives.

India

IN EAST AFRICA, THE THOUGHT OF VISITING INDIA HAD never occurred to most of us third-generation Asians. We simply went about our business. Although Bollywood movies were very popular, with their depictions of poverty and opulence, their portrayals of the disparities in Indian society, we had no connection with India except that our ancestors hailed from there. But now, in 2001, after twenty-nine years in Canada, I felt as if India was calling: my wife and I had this great urge to see our ancestral homeland. For me personally, a visit also had a special meaning: I had studied Indian history during my early days at Lindi Indian Public School. I was familiar with the great Mughal emperors, their famous historical monuments, and their grand empires. I now wanted to see where this history had been written.

As our plane descended into Indira Gandhi International Airport in New Delhi, my anxiety and emotions heightened. I was finally going to step on the soil of my ancestors. If the plane had not parked at the gate, I would have been tempted to kiss the ground. The airport was busy, and the air was misty, foggy, and full of dust-like particles. Our tour operator had sent a vehicle to receive us, which made it easier to get to our hotel.

We found Delhi to be a city of contrasts, made up of many blended cultures. We found Muslim shopkeepers in the Chandni Chowk area of Old Delhi, Tibetans and Ladakhis along Janpath, and Kashmiris in the handicraft emporia around Connaught Place, all adding to the cosmopolitan feel of the city. The most powerful emperors in Indian history had ruled from the old section, while New Delhi—a small district in the greater metropolitan area—had become the capital of British India in 1911 and then the seat of the Indian government after independence in 1947. Delhi is a garden city, featuring many parks. It also boasts three UNESCO World Heritage Sites: Qutub Minar, the Red Fort, and Humayun's Tomb. But one of the most popular sites in New Delhi is Raj Ghat, the memorial to the great Mahatma Gandhi that marks the place of his cremation. The site is on the itinerary of every foreign head of state visiting India.

One of the first things that amazed me when we started our sightseeing tour in Delhi was the traffic in the city. Cars, scooters, motorbikes, bicycles, rickshaws, and cows clogged the streets, and the cows—considered sacred among Hindus—had the right-of-way. It was very common to see traffic stopping to allow them to cross the streets while average pedestrians were granted no quarter. Judging from the snail's pace at which the cows crossed the streets, it seemed as if they were aware of their special privilege.

It also appeared that no one observed any traffic laws—people drove in any fashion they wanted to. But despite this, the heavy traffic, and the overcrowded streets, we didn't notice any accidents during our visit.

After four days in New Delhi we flew to Varanasi, the ultimate pilgrimage spot for Hindus. Also known as Benares or Kashi, Varanasi is one of the oldest living cities in the world. Hindus believe that one who is graced to die on the land of Varanasi may attain salvation and freedom from the cycle of birth and rebirth. Considered a symbol of Hindu renaissance, Varanasi has flourished as a centre of knowledge, philosophy, culture, and devotion to gods, Indian arts, and crafts.

The next stop on our trip was the mystic Khajuraho, a small town made famous for the graphic representation of sexual and erotic postures on the walls of its temples. The beautiful sculptures have gained the attention of art lovers all over the world—and are also recognized as a UNESCO World Heritage Site—but the reason for their existence is anyone's guess.

We were then on to Agra to see the Taj Mahal, one of the "new" seven wonders of the world. No visit to India is complete without seeing it. Built by the Mughal emperor Shah Jahan as a tribute to his wife, Mumtaz, the site attracts millions of visitors every year.

After Agra, we travelled to Mumbai, which has been described as ancient yet modern. Known as Bombay until 1995, and considered the gateway to India, Mumbai originally consisted of seven islands, which were joined together by a series of reclamations. We were warned about the paradox of Mumbai, with its grinding poverty and its ostentatious wealth. It is the financial and business capital of India, as well as the centre of Hindi film industry. Known as Bollywood and famous worldwide, it is one of the biggest film industries of the world, producing over one thousand films every year.

Our taxi driver, a Muslim named Farouq who had lived in Mumbai all his life, proved to be an interesting man, philosophical about the relations between India's dominant populations. He said he never had problems with Hindus, adding, "It's a great tragedy that this land of Muslim Mughal emperors and Indian maharajahs has seen so much bloodshed over Kashmir. For the most part, Hindus and Muslims in India have lived together in harmony, and the Kashmiris should learn from us." He also pointed out that the Muslim Mughal emperors had built famous landmarks throughout India, thus enriching the history, culture, and traditions of the country. "The Hindus should be grateful to the Mughal emperors for leaving behind such a rich legacy—these monuments have been earning revenue for the Indian government for years," he said.

Tragically, Hindu-Muslim antagonism is often exploited by the country's film industry: many Bollywood films depict Muslims as villains or bad guys. Pakistan, whose film industry is not as advanced as Bollywood's, is at a loss to retaliate in the same fashion.

On the last leg of our tour, we had arranged to spend three days in Goa, the beach capital of India, to relax before heading home. When we arrived in Goa, I mentioned to our driver on the way to the hotel from the airport that I wanted to buy a bottle of Scotch. "No problem, sir!" I was told. After a few minutes, the vehicle stopped at a tailor's shop. Thinking that the driver had misunderstood me, I repeated my request. But he told me to follow him into the shop, where we found a tailor sitting behind a sewing machine, the front of which was covered with a cloth curtain. The driver told the man what I wanted. From behind the curtain, the tailor took out several bottles of Scotch, displaying various brands for my perusal. I made my choice and paid him. Back in the car I asked the driver why the tailor was selling liquor. I was told that it was his part-time business. He bought liquor from Goans returning from abroad and then resold it to tourists at a markup.

Goa—a Portuguese enclave for 450 years until 1961, when the Portuguese were militarily ejected—has its own unique architecture, lifestyle, and cuisine, the latter considered to be one of the best in India. It was a real treat for me to have fish cooked Goan style for lunch, after a swim and a refreshing cold beer.

During our three-week "pilgrimage" to India in 2001, I found myself quite at ease, spiritually and mentally. Having lived first in a black-dominated society in Africa and now in a white-dominated society in Canada, I found a complete absence of racial tension when going about on the street in India. I was at ease everywhere I went, with none of the fear, panic, or insults that I had encountered in some situations in Canada and Africa. I was communally anonymous. The experience was remarkable; everyone on the street was brown in colour and there was no chance of anyone calling me a "Paki" or a *muhindi*. I found myself submerged in the brown ocean of humanity. It was an incredible experience. This trip to India opened my eyes: racism was completely absent on the streets, and for the first time in my life I was not considered a visible minority.

* * *

In 2011, ten years after my first trip to India, and at the ripe age of sixty-eight, I decided to visit the country again, this time to see my ancestral home in the state of Gujarat. My paternal grandfather had come from the small village of Bhadreshwar, on the Gulf of Kutch, a four-hour drive southeast of Bhuj, one of the major cities in the state.

Just getting to Bhadreshwar was quite an experience for Anaar and me. We had to travel on unpaved roads through several villages, manoeuvring through trucks, cars, motorbikes, bicycles, rickshaws, cows, and the pedestrians who braved all this traffic. Again, drivers in India do not follow any traffic rules or signals—they just go.

When we finally arrived in Bhadreshwar, it was quite emotional. I again felt like kissing the ground (like the late Pope John Paul II used to do when visiting foreign countries), but the dirty street and the cow dung everywhere made me change my mind. Our guide, Jamsheed, went to the *mukhi*, the head of the village, to inquire about the whereabouts of my ancestors, or any descendants of relatives that my grandfather would have left behind. To my utter disappointment, we were informed that they had long left the village. Someone knew where they lived; however, I had to content myself with looking at what had been their residence.

The visit to Bhadreshwar made me think of my ancestors living there in the 1800s, and I visualized their life in this impoverished area, undergoing a tough existence. If my grandfather hadn't left for Africa, I figured I would have been one of the farmers tilling the land or shepherds tending a herd of sheep in this mainly agricultural area. Even today, the village has no industries; there is only one small shop where people buy food and other necessities. A travelling salesman who was passing through at the time of my visit made periodic sales trips to the community so that the shopkeeper can buy his stock. Even though the people of Gujarat are gregariously friendly and inviting and will entice you to come again and again, I couldn't imagine myself living in Bhadreshwar today.

The decision of my grandfather and others like him to leave India for East Africa to seek better lives for their children and grandchildren had certainly been the right one. We received a good education, had good upbringings, and had opportunities that those left behind in India never dreamt of. As such, we were well equipped to undergo a second migration decades later, to Canada, the United States, and Europe, again to seek a new homeland and brighter future for our children.

In the first migration, India's loss was Africa's gain, but in the second migration, it was Africa's loss and the West's gain—and my gain, too. When I arrived back in Canada after my second trip to India, I again felt like kissing the ground, but this time the ground that had become my home.

Fifty Years after Nyerere

ON DECEMBER 9, 2011, TANZANIA—SO NAMED AFTER TANganyika merged with the island of Zanzibar in 1964—celebrated its fiftieth anniversary of independence amid pomp and festivities. In the half century since it shed its colonial shackles in 1961, the country has had a rough ride. President Julius Nyerere garnered world attention by following an aggressive policy of socialism, taking an outspoken stand on foreign policy, and offering unreserved support for Pan-Africanism. Nyerere believed that no country in Africa was free until all African nations were independent. Freedom fighters and liberation organizations from Mozambique, Zimbabwe, South Africa, Angola, and South West Africa converged on Dar es Salaam, Tanzania's capital, making it the headquarters of Africa's freedom movement.

Nyerere used Tanzania as a pulpit to spread his socialist philosophy, and as a university student in the 1960s, I worshipped the man. I admired him for squaring off against the United States and the colonial power, Britain, to try and create a just society. But by the late 1960s Tanzania had become one of the world's poorest countries, suffering from a severe foreign debt, a decrease in foreign aid, and a fall in the price of exported commodities. Nyerere's solution involved the collectivization of agriculture, villagization, and large-scale nationalization. This vision, set out in the Arusha Declaration of 1967, was a unique blend of socialism, collectivism, and communal life, called *ujamaa*.

As I said earlier, I had the privilege of meeting Nyerere, first as a student leader and later as a journalist, and my adulation for him never diminished. When he retired in 1985, stepping down as president after twenty-four years, he was only the third modern African head of state to relinquish power voluntarily while in office. Although his socialist experiment failed, Nyerere, who died of leukemia on October 14, 1999, will be remembered as a man dedicated to his countrymen, who wanted to develop his country without depending on Western aid.

It was left to the succeeding leadership in Tanzania to dismantle government controls over the economy—meaning reversing Nyerere's policies—and this tremendous task fell upon three of his successors: Ali Hassan Mwinyi (1985–1995), Benjamin Mkapa (1995–2005), and Jakaya Kikwete (2005–2015). It took these three presidents to undo what Nyerere had done.

During Mwinyi's terms as president, Tanzania relaxed import restrictions and encouraged private enterprise. Mwinyi also introduced multi-party politics. The next president, Mkapa, privatized state-owned corporations and instituted free-market policies, arguing that attracting foreign investment would promote economic growth. Kikwete's government then received accolades for fighting corruption, investing in people and in education, and pushing for continued economic liberalization.

Kikwete's government steered the country through challenging times, domestically, regionally, and globally. One of his government's main strategies was to develop agriculture, as 75 percent of Tanzanians live in rural areas and survive by working the land. Kikwete also oversaw real improvements in health and education services. Today, 97 percent of children are in primary school, compared to only 2 percent at the time of independence. There had been only thirteen university graduates by the time of independence; presently, over 120,000 students are studying at various universities in the country. In the health sector, much was done to increase people's access to health care and to combat diseases. There are now more dispensaries, health centres, and hospitals in Tanzania's villages, districts, and regions.

Kikwete also had a significant role to play regionally. As chair of the African Union in 2008, he was a key figure in peace talks that brought about a resolution to a violent political dispute in neighbouring Kenya. Additionally, as an advocate for an economic free zone among its neighbours, Tanzania under Kikwete formed a customs union with four other member states—Kenya, Uganda, Rwanda, and Burundi—in 2010.

Today, Tanzania—a nation of 126 tribes who belong to different races, religions, and backgrounds—is considered to be one of Africa's most politically stable countries.

* * *

After fifty years of independence, Tanzania's political leadership realized the potential of its Asian diaspora to help with the development of the country. In 2012, I was among three hundred expatriates who gathered in Edmonton to hear President Kikwete appeal to his country's former citizens. The president, who led a high-powered delegation consisting of ministers, ambassadors, and heads of leading banks and government departments, urged Tanzanians living in Canada to return home, to invest in the country, and to use their skills and knowledge to help with the growth and development of their former homeland. Kikwete assured the delegates, including people whose homes, properties, and businesses had been nationalized under Nyerere, that Tanzania was open for business, promising that "there [would] be no more nationalization."

Kikwete rolled out the welcome mat, saying Tanzania was encouraging a market economy based upon private-sector investment. He added that the government had recognized the private sector was the "engine of growth," and further, had realized its role was to govern, maintain law and order, and provide a healthy environment for business.

Addressing his audience, which included successful businesspeople, hoteliers, community leaders, and professionals—Asian Tanzanians then residing in Canada—President Kikwete assured them that they had left the country under "different" circumstances. "Those times are gone," he said. However, a questioner was disappointed when he was bluntly told that properties nationalized under Nyerere would not be returned or compensated for, as was done under President Museveni in Uganda.

In a later interview with me, one skeptical Asian businessman questioned whether or not expatriates could trust the Tanzanian politicians. "Mr. Kikwete can guarantee what is happening during his term of office," he said, adding, "Three or four years down the road, he'll be gone. Can he guarantee what his successor is going to do?"

Another Asian, whose family had lost properties under Nyerere, said if the government was serious, it would return nationalized properties as was done in Uganda as an act of good faith. "The fact that they said no to returning them shows they are a bunch of thieves who want to keep someone else's properties," he remarked.

So important were Tanzanian expatriates living abroad that the government formed a specific Diaspora Department under its Ministry of Foreign Affairs, with the goal of enticing the diaspora to contribute to the socioeconomic, political, and cultural development of the country. Tanzanians living in Alberta were specifically urged to make a special effort to return home to boost the country's economy, since Tanzania needed their expertise in oil and gas. "You have the experience and skills that we need," Kikwete stated. The president also identified mining, tourism, telecommunications, manufacturing, and construction as areas of great opportunity. "We need investors. Come and invest," Kikwete urged. "We need technology and skills. . . . Don't forget home, sweet home."

Kikwete then invited the present members of the Tanzanian Asian diaspora to share their views on the drafting of a new constitution. Five decades after independence, the government saw the need to bring it up to speed with present realities. The president also stated that the country was looking at ways to offer dual nationality to Tanzanians living abroad. Decades ago, the country turned its back on us; now we were being welcomed back.

Return to Africa

IN 2015, AFTER AN ABSENCE OF MORE THAN FOUR DECADES, I was at long last able to visit my former homeland. Wherever I went I heard the song "Hakuna Matata," a popular Swahili song, the title of which, literally translated, means "no problem" or "no trouble." I heard this song at every hotel and resort, and any other place that catered to tourists. Entertainers loved to play this song for visitors to the country, and recordings of it were offered as a souvenir to take home. It appeared as if the song was reflecting the desire of the nation: to show that there was no problem with its drive towards economic growth and political liberalization.

Indeed, growth and development were evident in every corner of Dar es Salaam. Construction companies were doing a booming business, and new buildings were springing up to replace old ones. In the 1970s, the tallest building in the country was an eleven-storey structure in Dar called Mawingu (clouds), owned by an Asian businessman. Today the city's skyline has completely changed, with several skyscrapers reaching thirty to forty storeys in height. According to the International Monetary Fund, the Tanzanian economy went through a period of successful transition over the last two decades, and the country has seen significant growth in its gross domestic product.

I found Dar's streets congested with people and heavy traffic. People and cars were everywhere. Traffic jams, especially during rush hours, are the norm. A businessman friend purposely leaves his business early, at 3:00 p.m., in order to reach his home at a decent hour. The Africa Development Bank has predicted that the city's current population of 1.14 million will grow by more than 85 percent through 2025, reaching 21.4 million by 2052, making Dar one of the world's fastest-growing cities. The government, however, appears to be ill prepared for the demands that will be placed on the city's infrastructure.

A pleasant observation for me, though, was to see the local newspapers thriving. Newspaper stands were at every corner, each selling several English and Swahili papers. Nothing pleased me more than seeing people reading the local papers on the streets and in restaurants. The

British-owned daily, the *Standard*—where I had begun my career as a journalist and which was nationalized by Nyerere in 1970—was still in business, although it has been renamed the *Daily News*. A more prominent English-language daily, the *Citizen*, owned by the Aga Khan's Nairobi-based Nation Media Group, has taken the lead in readership and circulation, however. I also noted that Tanzanians are more vocal today than they had been during Nyerere's time. They now openly criticize government programs and corrupt politicians without fear. I could easily sense the public opinion by reading letters to the editor in newspapers, and I had a good feeling that the political leadership, which now accepts such criticism, has reached maturity.

I also observed that the Chinese had replaced local Indians as the dominant business community in Tanzania. People of Chinese origin, despite outcries by some local Africans, now operated many, many businesses in Dar. A survey undertaken by a local daily found that Kariakoo—Dar's main market for produce, meat, and vegetables, and at one time almost exclusively an African enclave—was fast on its way to becoming Chinatown.

During my 2015 visit, Tanzanian president Jakaya Kikwete unveiled a new education policy for the country, which made Swahili the medium of instruction from primary school to university, thereby replacing English, the dominant language for the education system for close to a century. The policy was applauded by party stalwarts and nationalist-minded citizens, but critics doubted whether replacing English with Swahili was the right thing to do. As it stood, the country had an acute shortage both of Swahili books and of experts proficient enough to produce books to satisfy the demand or teach the language properly. It was also a known fact that practically no demand for Swahili-speaking graduates would exist outside of Tanzania.

During my visit I also became keenly aware of political tension with Zanzibar on the horizon. Zanzibar, where I was born, already has its own president and Parliament, as it has a semi-autonomous relationship with Tanzania, but an increasing number of Zanzibaris are anxious to separate from the mainland. As a popular tourist destination, Zanzibar earns plenty of foreign exchange and many islanders feel that they could stand on their own.

As my trip back to Tanzania came to an end, I found myself with mixed emotions. When you grow up in a certain place, you take everything for granted. You also find it mundane because that is all you know. But if you leave and return after a prolonged period—again, over forty years in my case—you see the place with different eyes.

Tanzania is wonderful and exotic, but however enchanting it is, I realized with great sadness that it could never be my home again. Canada, a country whose values I cherish with pride, is and will continue to be my home. Zanzibar is my birthplace, and Tanzania the place where I grew up, but Canada will be my final resting place.

Diaspora Lament

I HAVE BEEN IN CANADA FOR OVER FORTY-FIVE YEARS now, but I am still asked about my nationality at practically every cocktail party I go to. The question is a routine conversation opener.

When I respond that I am a Canadian, the person then smiles and says, "I mean, where do you originally come from?"

"From Tanzania," I respond.

"Is that in South Africa?"

"No, in East Africa, near Kenya and Idi Amin's Uganda." Everyone by now has heard of the infamous dictator.

"But you are not black."

"You are right. My ancestors came from India and settled in what was Tanganyika at the time. I was of the third generation born in Africa."

Then almost the whole evening is taken up explaining the history of how Asians first came to the shores of East Africa, how they contributed to opening up trade and commerce on the continent, and how they ended up being persecuted and having to flee the countries of their birth.

And so it goes. Despite having Canadian citizenship, and despite having lived in Canada for over forty-five years, I still have to explain my being here. Such conversations generate a feeling of not quite being accepted. And part of it obviously has to do with the colour of my skin. This was painfully evident when someone on the street in Edmonton once (very succinctly) yelled at me, "Paki, go back where you came from!" It was deeply hurtful, and I was flabbergasted. I was supposedly in one of the most multiethnic, multicultural, and diverse cities in Canada. Yes, the bigot's remark was stupid—I am not from Pakistan (not that there is anything wrong with being from Pakistan)—but his callous affront made me think hard.

His comment, "Go back where you came from," led me to ask myself a question: Just where *am* I from? Dar es Salaam, where I lived through my most formative years? Or Zanzibar, where my parents and I were born? Or India, where my ancestors came from? Just where is my homeland? I wondered. Do I have one? It was the first time I had really given any thought to the importance of a homeland.

And I realized that one does not recognize how important it is until one is either fighting for acceptance or displaced.

A homeland is defined as one's native land or country of origin. It is where an ethnic group has a long history and a deep cultural association. In the case of the *muhindi*, I wondered, is our homeland India or Africa? Or might it be possible for us to have a new homeland—in the new countries where we have now lived for decades, where we have built our lives, to which we have sworn our allegiance? Our origins were in India, we had a long history in and deep cultural and emotional ties with Africa, but now many of us are firmly ensconced in the West, in countries where we have raised our children, and where our grandchildren have been born. My son, Hanif, is as Canadian as anyone else. Could Canada possibly be *his* homeland? Should he be asked about his nationality at the cocktail parties he attends?

In the early 1970s, when the Asian exodus out of East Africa took place, we expected India and Pakistan, our kith and kin, to be the first countries to open their doors to us, but they weren't. Yes, they accepted token numbers of us—India and Pakistan each took three thousand of their "nationals"—but no more. To their credit, it was so-called white nations—Canada, the United States, Britain—who came to our rescue. So, when I was called a Paki in Edmonton, I was deeply disturbed. I had thought I was welcome in this country, I was trying to make it my home, when some idiot put a dent in my dreams. Demoralized, I told my parents about the incident.

My father, who listened patiently, responded, "You realize the Africans threw us out of East Africa and we came here virtually penniless. People from Uganda didn't have anything; they also came to Canada penniless. Look at them now. They have cars, homes, and comfortable lives. The whites have allowed us to stay in their country. They opened their doors to us.

"Not all the whites are so bad," he continued. "At least they won't nationalize our properties and homes like those blacks did," he added, recalling his own experience of losing his property. "I can sleep here soundly without any worries. You remember Uncle Janu in Dar es Salaam? They suspected him of doing something, and they placed him in jail without trial for almost a year. Things like that don't happen here. There is safety for a person and rule of law."

Now I listened patiently. "Yes, some stupid people don't like us because we're brown—so what? There are thousands who don't hate us. Think of this wonderful life and thank God for it. Don't be discouraged, son, because one guy abused you on the street. Canada has been good to us."

I calmed down, but a question still lingered in my mind: Will we ever be fully accepted here? Will our children, or their children? Will the colour of one's skin always be an issue? That's the multimillion-dollar question. The day people are accepted as Canadians regardless of whether they are black, brown, beige, or whatever, then I will truly feel that my coming to Canada was fully worthwhile.

Many times, I have dreamt that the world should be a borderless frontier, where every man, woman, and child is accepted as an equal human being, where citizenship, ethnicity, and colour are irrelevant. So far this remains a dream. I do not want to be a dweller of several lands, accepted by none.

Postscript

IN HIS LATER YEARS DAD BECAME SICK AND WAS HOSPITALIZED. Doctors in the family—my brother Shiraz and his wife, Gwen—kept in constant touch with Dad's doctors in Canada, but unfortunately, on July 2, 1989, Dad passed away. Mom decided to live by herself at first, but then she was struck with Alzheimer's disease and we had to move her into a facility in west Edmonton. The facility, especially for Alzheimer patients, provided outings and activities. Mom enjoyed her stay there, especially the extracurricular activities. One evening, I went to visit her and, to my amazement, she was in the social hall dancing. She blushed when I teased her about her new "boyfriend"—her dance partner.

She then had a fall that resulted in her needing to use a wheelchair. According to the facility's rules, patients had to be independently mobile; those unable to do so were forced to move out. Mom was transferred to a seniors' home.

As time went by, she became more confused, losing track of time and unable to do simple things. Seeing her deteriorate gradually from Alzheimer's was a sad part of my life. Later it became unbearable to visit her because she couldn't even recognize members of the family. She also started muttering unintelligible words, making no sense, while we sat there listening to her with tears in our eyes. She passed away on November 15, 2006, surrounded by all her children. I salute my parents for the upbringing and good life that they gave us. Three of their five children completed a university education, while the other two went on to sound careers.

We learned a lot from these tough old veterans.

Notes

1. Paul Theroux, "Hating the Asians," *Transition*, no. 33 (1967): 46.
2. Ibid.
3. Jean Allman, *Fashioning Africa: Power and the Politics of Dress* (Bloomington: Indiana University Press, 2004), 105.
4. Peter Tweedy, letter to the editor, *Standard*, October 17, 1968.
5. Haroub Othman, "Mwalimu Julius Nyerere: An Intellectual in Power," in *Yes, In My Lifetime: Selected Works of Haroub Othman*, ed. Saida Yahya-Othman (Dar es Salaam: Mkuki na Nyota), 98.
6. Anthony Lestor, "East African Asians versus the United Kingdom: The Inside Story" (lecture, Odysseus Trust, London, October 23, 2003), www.odysseustrust.org/lectures/221_east_african_asians-sharma.pdf.
7. David Martin, *General Amin* (London: Faber & Faber, 1974).
8. Ibid.

THE REGINA COLLECTION

Named as a tribute to Saskatchewan's capital city with its rich history of boundary-defying innovation, The Regina Collection builds upon University of Regina Press's motto of "a voice for many peoples." Intimate in size and beautifully packaged, these books aim to tell the stories of those who have been caught up in social and political circumstances beyond their control.

Other books in *The Regina Collection:*

Time Will Say Nothing:
A Philosopher Survives an Iranian Prison
by Ramin Jahanbegloo (2014)

The Education of Augie Merasty:
A Residential School Memoir
by Joseph Auguste Merasty,
with David Carpenter (2015)

Inside the Mental:
Silence, Stigma, Psychiatry, and LSD
by Kay Parley (2016)

Otto & Daria:
A Wartime Journey through No Man's Land
by Eric Koch (2016)

Towards A Prairie Atonement
by Trevor Herriot, afterword by Norman Fleury (2016)

ABOUT MANSOOR LADHA

An award-winning journalist, Mansoor Ladha has held several senior editorial positions at daily and weekly newspapers in Canada, Tanzania, and Kenya. He has also freelanced for the *Calgary Herald*, *Vancouver Sun*, *Edmonton Journal*, *Lethbridge Herald*, *Medicine Hat News*, *Kerby News*, several weeklies, and travel magazines. He is the author of *A Portrait in Pluralism: Aga Khan's Shia Ismaili Muslims*.

He received the Citizen of the Year Award from the Town of Morinville in 2005; the Silver Quill Award, for distinguished service to the newspaper industry, from the Alberta Weekly Newspapers Association in 2011; and the Governor General's Caring Canadian Award in 2013 (now called the Sovereign's Medal for Volunteers). He currently lives in Calgary.